THE INDIANS OF PUGET SOUND

by

HERMANN HAEBERLIN and ERNA GUNTHER

UNIVERSITY OF WASHINGTON PRESS

SEATTLE AND LONDON

Published as Volume IV, Number 1, of the University of Washington
Publications in Anthropology, 1930
Library of Congress Catalog Card Number 30-27636
ISBN 0–295–73813–8
Second printing, 1952
Third printing, 1956
Fourth printing, 1959
Fifth printing, 1962
Sixth printing, 1965
Seventh printing, 1967
Eighth printing, 1971
Ninth printing, 1973
Tenth printing, 1975
Eleventh printing, 1977
Twelfth printing, 1980
Printed in the United States of America

PREFACE

This paper was originally printed in the Zeitschrift für Ethnologie, Jahrgang 1924, Heft 1-4, and acknowledgment is hereby made to that journal for their courtesy in permitting this reprinting. The monograph deals principally with the Snohomish and Snuqualmi tribes now concentrated on the Tulalip Reservation, Washington, and who formerly occupied the valleys of the rivers that bear their names. Since the original publication of the paper, the present writer has gone over some of Dr. Haeberlin's ground and made a few revisions and changes. It has been almost impossible to add much material, for Dr. Haeberlin worked with the oldest people available in 1916-1917 and since then most of them have died. There has been no active participation in the culture described here for well over fifty years, making it therefore all the more remarkable that Dr. Haeberlin was able to salvage so much. The information on the guardian spirits and shamanistic spirits is especially fine, and can never be obtained again.

The opportunity of reprinting this paper in the University of Washington publications is greatly appreciated, for it will doubtless be more accessible to students of Northwest ethnography.

ERNA GUNTHER

University of Washington
July 15, 1930.

CONTENTS

Page

Preface 3

Introduction 7
    Tribes described 7
    Location 7
    Characteristics 10
    Intertribal relations 11

Villages and Houses 15
    The village 15
    Winter houses 15
    Summer houses 18

Economic Life 20
    Varieties and Preparation of food. 20
    Fire making 24
    Hunting 25
    Fishing 26
    Money and Money Values. 29
    Values and Measurements 29

Crafts 30
    Weaving 30
    Cedar bark shredding 32
    Mats 32
    Basketry 32
    Skinwork 33
    Tools 33
    Wood work 34

Dress and Personal Care. 37
    Dress 37
    Personal care 39
    Sweat lodges 41

Life of the Individual. 43
    Birth Customs 43
    Puberty Ceremonies 45
    Names 46
    Instruction of Children 48
    Menstrual Customs 49
    Marriage 50
    Burial and Mourning Customs. 53

Social Life of the Group. 56
    Social Grouping 56
    Kinship Terms 56
    Slavery 57
    Government 58
    Group gatherings 59
    Diversions 62
    Smoking 66

Religious Life 67
    The Guardian Spirit Concept 67
    Sklaletut Spirits 69
    Shamanism 75
    Dreams 80
    Ghosts and Souls 81

Bibliography 82

FIGURES

I. Distribution of Puget Sound Tribes. 8
II. Salmon Trap 27
III. Roller Loom for Salish Mountain Blanket. 31

THE INDIANS OF PUGET SOUND

INTRODUCTION

TRIBES DESCRIBED

The tribes which are the most fully described in these notes are the Snohomish, the Snuqualmi and the Nisqually. There is some information about the Skykomish and Skagit, while casual references are made to many other Puget Sound groups. The three principal groups involved speak dialects of Coast Salish that are very nearly alike. The Snohomish and Snuqualmi now reside on the Tulalip Reservation, Washington, where Dr. Haeberlin did the larger part of his work. There are also quite a number of Snuqualmi in the neighborhood of Tolt, which was the center of their old territory, and another scattering is on the Muckleshoot Reservation south of Seattle. The situation that existed in aboriginal conditions in regard to residence still holds, namely that with tribal exogamy and patrilocal residence there is considerable heterogeneity in every community.

LOCATION

The Snohomish lived in four principal villages. Hēbō′lb on the shores of the Sound, four miles south of Tulalip; Tc′iʟ!ā′qs, the largest village, at Priest Point; nɛgᵘā′sx on the southern point of Whidby Island; and Tcɛtcɬqs at Sandy Point, opposite Tulalip.[1] The Snohomish claim that Hēbō′lb is their original home, because the transformer, Dokᵘibeɫ, put them there when he came to Mukilteo and changed everything. For hunting and fishing they roamed through the territory to the east of these villages. Tangible evidence of their occupation of the Snohomish River valley exists at Ebey's Slough on the westernmost branch of the Snohomish River about two miles from Marysville. On the right bank of the stream is a shell heap, six feet high and one quarter mile long.[2] No effort has been made to excavate it.

The Snoqualmie (sdōkwā′lbixᵘ) lived on the Snoqualmie River from North Bend to the junction of the Skykomish and the Snoqualmie rivers.[3] In summer they went to Snoqualmie Prairie to gather roots and berries and roamed through the Cascade Mountains hunting.

The Nisqually[4] (sqolē′abc) occupied a large territory extending from the head of the Sound to the east of Mt. Rainier.[5] At the time of the war with the

---

[1] These locations agree in general with those cited by Bancroft from the old railroad exploration report. Bancroft, I, 300; Handbook, 606; Gibbs, (b) 432.

[2] This shell heap is on land belonging to Edward Perceval, one of Dr. Haeberlin's informants.

[3] "Reside on South fork, north side of the Sinahomish (Snohomish) River," Stevens in Bancroft, I, 300. "Upper branches of a river of the same name," Handbook, 606.

[4] Nisqually is supposed to be derived from the French, nez qarrées; the French regarded the noses of the Squally as unusually flat (square).

[5] Located on Nisqually River south of the Puyallups, about Olympia and some of the bays to the west. Eells, (b) 9. "de la baie de Puget a la pointe Martinez," Mofras in Bancroft, I, 301. All authorities agree on the location around the Nisqually River.

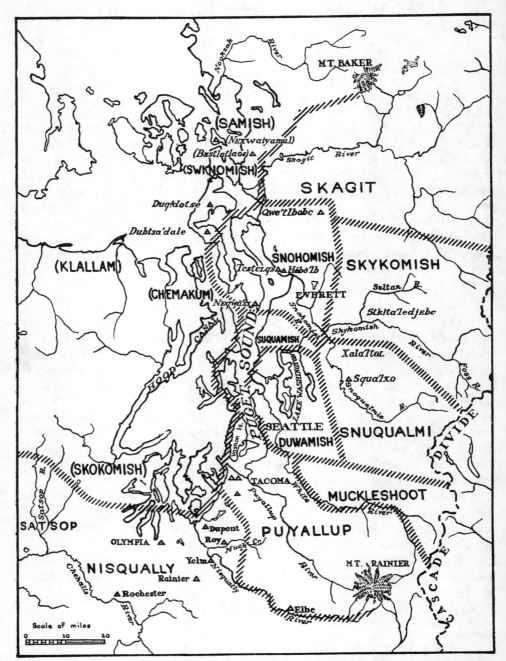

Fig. I. Distribution of Puget Sound Tribes. (Triangles indicate Indian villages. Tribes and settlements in parentheses are not discussed in this paper, but occupy contiguous territory.)

whites (1855-56) there were, according to Henry Sicade, about 2000 Nisqually.[6] Ten villages were enumerated for the Nisqually; the head village was located at the junction of Muck Creek and the Nisqually River. The other villages, designated by the modern towns now standing on old village sites, were: Hillcrest, Yelm, Rainier, near Roy, South Tacoma, Dupont, Olympia, Elbe, Rachester. The Nisqually often travelled east of the Mountains using Cowlitz and Naches Passes. The Nisqually River is excellent for winter fishing. This, the Nisqually shared with the Puyallup. The two tribes also had joint berry picking grounds. The Satsep, sometimes regarded as a distinct tribe, are a band of Nisqually who lived on Satsep Creek and intermarried with the Chehalis and Skykomish.

The Skykomish (Skī'xobc), called squqō'mc by the Snohomish, lived along the Skykomish and Foss Rivers. A band of Skykomish called Stk!ta'ledjɛbc used to live on Sultan Creek; they are extinct now.[7] All the Skykomish wandered through the Cascade Mountains on hunting expeditions. They are also called sq!ē'wabc and sq!ē'xob.

The Skagit lived in two groups, one at Niccolum Point (tcōba'a'lcɛd), and the other further away from Tulalip at Bā"asats.[8] The three chiefs of the Skagit lived at Niccolum Point. They were Kwau'qēd, Sʟ!asxō' and a third whose name was not obtained. Dokᵘibɛɫ changed them into tiō'ɫbax spirits.

The Puyallup (spuya'lupo'bc) lived along the banks of the Puyallup and White Rivers, including the present site of Tacoma and Point Defiance. They also occupied the whole of Vashon Island.[9] Their territory was much smaller than that of the Nisqually. The main village was situated on the north bank of the Puyallup River near Cushman School. At the City Waterway of Tacoma the medicine house of the tribe stood and on the north side of the bay, opposite the Tacoma Hotel was the great potlatch house. There was a village at Brown's Point. Numerous villages were scattered over the prairie at North Puyallup and there was a continuous line of small settlements from the present Tacoma Hotel to the Stadium.

The Muckleshoot (o'kɛlcuɫ) lived on the White River, their territory extending from Kent east to the mountains. Just east of the Muckleshoot and the Nisqually lived the Klikitat, whose lands extended south to the Columbia River and eastward to the mountains.[10] The Klikitat in family groups crossed the mountains once a year in July or August, using Cowlitz Pass. There is a stream near the

---

[6] Nisqually population, 1844, 563; 1878, 278; 1910, 137. Eells, (d) 272; Census 1910, 19.

[7] Jack Wheeler, an informant, was partly Stk!ta'lēdjɛbc.

[8] The Skagit lived along the Skagit River in five bands, one of which was the Swinomish. Eells (b) 8. To the above location Bancroft adds Steven's note of Skagit territory on Whidby Island near Penn's Cove. Wilkes, Nicolay and Schoolcraft all bear out Stevens' statement. Bancroft, I, 299.

[9] Same territory defined. This became an important reservation because it is the most valuable on the Sound. Eells (b) 9. The authorities in Bancroft only name the Puyallup River territory. Bancroft, I, 301.

[10] The Klikitat and Yakima are supposed to have driven out the Salish tribes who once occupied these lands. Gibbs (a) 224. Between 1830 and 1855 the Klikitat settled along the Lewis River, the Willamette and the Umkwa. They were formerly in the eastern part of the state. *Ibid.*, 170.

waterworks in Tacoma called Swā'd abc meaning "Plains People," because the Klikitat used to travel along its banks down to the Sound. The Cowlitz occupied the country from the Columbia River north to the Squally territory. They were neighbors of the Chehalis in the west and of the Klikitat in the East. There are only a few people left now who can speak Cowlitz.

The Duwamish[11] (Duxᵘduwa'bc) lived about the present site of Seattle, their territory extending from the Muckleshoot lands in the south to the Suquamish territory in the north. They were also called Renton Indians.[12] The Suquamish (Suk!wa'bc), according to one informant, lived south of Everett, about Mukilteo and on the islands opposite; another claims that they lived only on the islands, west of Seattle and not around Mukilteo.[13] The Chehalis lived on the lower part of the Chehalis River from Centralia to Gray's Harbor.[14] The Shoalwater Indians lived south of Chehalis on the ocean.

CHARACTERISTICS

The Snohomish did not hunt deer and elk, so they bought the dressed skins from the Snuqualmi and paid for them with shell money. They made moccasins of these hides. They also bought mountain goat wool from the Snuqualmi and wove it into blankets. Before the coming of the whites, the Snohomish smoked kinnikinnik leaves.[15] They also obtained tobacco (sma'nac) from the Indians east of the mountains, before the advent of the whites. They bought pipes, made of a soft stone not found in Snohomish country, from the Yakima. They paid for both tobacco and pipe with shell money.

In summer the Snohomish left their large winter houses to go hunting and fishing. They did not leave their own lands, unless they had friends or relatives elsewhere. Although there were no sharp dividing lines between the territory of neighboring tribes, it was taken for granted that a person straying too far into the country of another tribe was looking for trouble. No date was set by the shamans or the chief for the spring migration. The people did not all go at once; the most energetic were the first to leave, the old people usually remaining at home. In summer two to ten families camped together in shelters covered with mats or brush. The man who caught the first salmon invited all his friends to a feast. Each one received a small piece of the salmon, but the host did not eat

---

[11] "Living on and claiming the land on the D'wamish River." Paige in Bancroft. "Duwamish River and Lake (Lake Duwamish, old name of Lake Washington), White and Green Rivers." Bancroft, I, 300.

[12] Lived on Dwamish River, tributaries, islands and peninsula to the west across the Sound. Some on Port Madison and Muckleshoot Reservations. Eells, (b) 8.

[13] "Claim all land lying on the west side of the Sound, between Apple Tree Cove and Gig Harbor." Others place them around Port Orchard and west side of Whidby Island and on peninsula between Hood's Canal and Admiralty Inlet. Bancroft, I, 301.

[14] Same territory defined. Eells, (b) 9.

[15] This statement by Edward Perceval is contradicted by Jules. Kinnikinnik leaves where not smoked alone, but mixed with tobacoo when the latter was scarce. Eells, (c) 213. The Indians of Shoalwater Bay dried the leaves of the bearberry bush (Arbutus uva ursi) and smoked them like tobacco. Swan, (a) 88.

any. Nobody was allowed to step over the first fish.[16] The same ceremony was carried out with the first deer, the first berries, and so forth.

In summer the Indians east of the mountains came to the coast to trade and get sea food for winter use. They used three passes to cross the mountains: the Cowlitz, the Snoqualmie and the Naches. The Klikitat used the Cowlitz, and the Wenatchee came through Snoqualmie.

INTERTRIBAL RELATIONS

The Nisqually called the Snuqualmi Snō'qwalbixᵘ, which means extraordinary people. They were said to be ferocious and warlike. They are supposed to be the only tribe who, previous to the coming of the whites, took the heads of their enemies as trophies. The Snuqualmi were also called stokᵘalmixᵘ, which means worthless people. "stokᵘ" means anything without value. Shelton said the Snuqualmi had a reputation for loose morals and general dishonesty. The Snuqualmi were great hunters and lived principally on game and salmon. They hunted in the mountains in winter, using snowshoes. They visited the Snohomish on the coast in summer, and while there they ate seal and sturgeon, but they never took these home because they did not keep.

About one hundred years ago many Nisqually emigrated to the Quinault and settled there. Sicade thinks that about one-half of the Quinault are of Nisqually descent. The two tribes are very friendly, notwithstanding the fact that their languages differ. When Sicade visited the Quinault they wanted to adopt him because they knew his grandfather. Many Nisqually spoke Klikitat and there were frequent intermarriages between the two tribes. The Cowichans and the Nisqually also intermarried. The Satsep, the group of Nisqually on Satsep Creek, have intermarried with the Chehalis and Skykomish.

In spite of the close relations between the Quinault and the Nisqually, these two tribes did not trade with one another. The Nisqually traded largely with the Klikitat, using shell money for payment. Shell money was highly prized by the Indians east of the mountains and the coast tribes used it more in trading with them than among themselves. The shell money which the Klikitat obtained from the Nisqually they in turn passed on to the Indians of Idaho and Montana. When the Klikitat came to the coast in summer they bought clams, herring, smelts and berries. In return they gave the Nisqually dried Columbia salmon, which is highly prized by the coast people.[17] They also brought dressed buckskins and clothing made of skins. The Nisqually never bought baskets from the Klikitat

---

[16] Saloon dances are found among the Yurok, Tolowa (Powers, 56, 67), and Chinook, who cut the meat of the fish with the grain and either burn or eat the heart. Bancroft, I, 232. The Chinook also cut the first salmon in small pieces and give each child in the village a piece. At the mouth of the Columbia River the shaman ate the first salmon, the heart being roasted and eaten, lest a dog get it. Gibbs adds that the Nisqually resemble the Chinook in all these practices. Gibbs, (a) 196. Swan, (a) 107. BAAS, 1890, 569. Discussion, Gunther, (b).

[17] The Dalles was a great center for trade, salmon trade particularly. Gibbs, (a) 195.

because they made better ones themselves, but the Klikitat bought coiled baskets from the Nisqually.

The Sound tribes seemed to have some knowledge of the people of the interior. They mentioned the stē'taɫ, identified by Teit as the Thompson. They believed that these tribes lived on the Fresh River. They called these people "wild tribes" who traveled by night and attacked lone wayfarers. They were cowards, never attacking larger groups, so they had no real wars with the Sound Indians. They spoke a language unintelligible to the Snohomish. The Sound Indians said that the stē'taɫ used to be savages but they had become civilized now.

Another tribe they mentioned are the qlō'sabc, which has not been identified. These people were supposed to be "savages" living in underground houses.[18] The Snohomish did not know exactly where the qlō'sabc lived permanently, for they roamed over the country most of the time. They were supposed to be "built like giants" and were noted for their thieving.

War. Some of the northern Indians, the Haida, Tsimshian and Makah, for example, were very warlike and frequently raided the Sound. They came down in their large war canoes. The Nisqually were comparatively safe from these raids, for they lived on the open prairie and could see the enemy approaching. The Sound tribes also waged war among themselves, and with the tribes in the immediate neighborhood. The Snohomish were foes of the Makah, Cowichans and Muckleshoot, but were friends of the Skagit, Suquamish, Duwamish, Klikitat, Skykomish, Lummi, Klallam and Nisqually. The Snuqualmi were friendly with the Snohomish and Skykomish and carried on war with the Cowichan, Klallam, and Nisqually. The Skykomish were at war with the Klikitat and Klallam, but were friends of the Snuqualmi and Snohomish.

These intertribal relations seemed to be more or less permanent, that is, whenever one tribe started war with another, the remaining tribes would line up according to these traditional relations of friend or foe. The causes of war are not enumerated. It is mentioned that a person with a warrior (duxᵘqlē'gwad) spirit can go to war any time he wants to, without asking the permission of the tribal chief. He proclaims to the people what spirit is prompting him and will help him in his venture. If a powerful man of one tribe murdered a man from another tribe, pride might induce him to refuse the payment that the murdered man's relatives demanded. This might lead to war.[19] Fishing, hunting and berry picking grounds were tribal property. One tribe could ask permission to use the territory of another, a favor which was rarely refused.[20] If, however, a tribe used the territory of another tribe without asking permission, the act was regarded as an invasion and war might follow.

---

[18] This fact leads one to believe that this was an interior Salish tribe, if it is not altogether mythical.
[19] Gibbs, (a) 190.
[20] Gibbs, (a) 186. "Some of the Lower Lillooet who were on good terms with the Lower Fraser Tribes were allowed to cross the Fraser River and hunt elk on its south side; but if strange Lillooet attempted to hunt there, they were driven off or killed." Teit, (a) 227, 236.

In time of war if the regular chief was not war-like, a war chief was selected.[21]   In the war with the whites, 1855-56, the Nisqually had lä'cai as war chief, but the regular chief Kitsap remained in authority, tending to affairs at home.   The war chief had supreme command, but, except in critical moments, he resorted to the council for advice and consent.   If a person resisted the will of the majority while the tribe was at war, the chief might punish him by giving him the hardest work, carrying provisions or making him fight in the front row, or, the hardest punishment of all, sending him home to the women and old people.   Capital punishment was only resorted to in war time as punishment for treason.   When starting out to war the chief took along only the courageous men. Often he induced men to go by giving them girls for wives or making presents of buckskins.

When the Snohomish heard rumors of an enemy's approach, they sent out young men as scouts.   If they saw the enemy they ran back and told their people. When the Snohomish at Hēbō'lb knew that foes were coming they sent messengers to the village at Priest Point.   The people of this village never fought; they fled to the woods.   The Snohomish never used fire signals such as those used by the Nisqually.   This tribe had signal stations at various points.   The last of these posts, (t atū'sō), was situated near the present Tacoma Hotel.

Many of the old villages were surrounded by walls.[22]   The most effective way of destroying such villages was to throw burning mats over the walls or to make pitchwood fires along the outside.

In war raids the men were killed and the women and children were enslaved.[23] The Snohomish never scalped their enemies.   The warriors brought home the heads of their victims to show the people, and then they threw them away.[24]

The Nisqually used bows and arrows, spears, flint and bone knives and war clubs.   The clubs (skwoi'ʟ!ᴇʟ) were made of elk horn, smoothed with a rough

---

[21] All war parties had war chiefs. Lillooet, Teit, (a) 235.
A war chief is elected by the warriors. Shuswap, BAAS 1890, 635.
The Thompson Indians had a war chief in command. Teit, (b) 267.

[22] The Tsimshian built stockades around houses for war. Boas, (b) 371, 536; Gibbs, (a) 192.   See Village, p. 15.   The Thompson Indians used no stockades but had a few fortified houses. Teit, (b) 266.

[23] Thompson, Teit, (b) 269.

[24] The Karok took heads. Powers, 21.
The Hupa cut off the heads of fallen enemies, but left them in the field. Powers, 74.
The Sound Indians stick the head of an enemy on a pole in front of their dwelling. Bancroft, I, 215.
There is mention of scalping among the Klallam. Bancroft, I, 215.
Tsimshian cut off heads of enemies and put them on poles. Also took scalps from heads. Boas, (b) 373.
Kwakiutl do the same as the Tsimshian. Boas, (a) 1016, 1374.
Lillooet do not scalp or behead. A few did it formerly and were said to have learned it from the Squamish of Howe Sound. Teit, (a) 235.
In the war with the whites in 1855 Patkanim, chief of the Snuqualmi, fought the Indians of White River on the side of the whites and brought to Colonel Simmons the heads of five Indians whom his party had slain. Swan, (a) 396. Scalping and beheading seems to have depended on individual fancy among the Thompson. Teit, (b) 268.

stone. Some were made of hard wood, but stone was never used.[25] Some tribes used poisoned arrows but according to Sicade, the Nisqually did not have them. Flint arrowheads were bought from the Snuqualmi, who were the only tribe that made them. A knife shaped like a dagger was also used. It was made of stone, sharpened on both sides. The handle was of horn and was riveted to the blade by means of horn pegs. The Snohomish used spears with polished stone points. They never had the cuirass.

It was said that the Snuqualmi and Snohomish had no war dance (sqwā'tsɛb). Yet at the time of the big potlatch in the autumn the Snohomish performed their war dance and each of the tribes that had been invited did the same.[26] In their war dance the Snohomish sang:

"I belong to the Snohomish tribe, I have no friends. I am a Snohomish." That means "I have killed all the people around here."

When a warrior killed an enemy he was not allowed to touch food with his fingers for ten days. He used a stick for eating. He also scratched his cheeks with a sharp stone to make them bleed; otherwise he would have a short life.[27]

[25] Another informant contradicts this statement by saying that Nisqually warriors carried two clubs made of black stone which were sharpened on one side only. The club had a hole in the handle through which a buck skin thong was fastened. By means of this thong the club was tied to the wrist. When using bow and arrow the club hung from the wrist. When not in action the warrior stuck the club through the back of his belt.

[26] It seems that formerly a war dance was performed in connection with war and later it was taken out of its own setting and used as an entertainment.

[27] Among the Lillooet a warrior who had killed an enemy had to paint his face black to avoid blindness. Teit, (a) 235.

VILLAGES AND HOUSES

THE VILLAGE

The Indians of Puget Sound always built their villages on the shores of the great water or along the rivers and creeks, with the houses facing the water and generally in a single row. The permanent villages occupied during the winter usually had from three to five large houses, together with a number of smaller ones.[28] Sometimes the village was protected by a palisade of cedar, about fourteen feet high.[29] Rocks were piled up at the base of the logs that were set about three feet into the ground. On top of the upright posts was laid a horizontal log grooved to fit the top of the uprights and tied to them with cedar rope. The palisade had doors of solid cedar planks barred on the inside with two horizontal beams. In addition to the doors, there were openings in the wall about one yard square for shooting arrows. These were cut at the height of a man's shoulder. These could also be closed from within by cedar boards that were bolted. These palisades enclosed the village on all sides including the water side. The burial ground was outside the wall.

The Snuqualmi and Skykomish did not have these palisades but the Skagit and Snohomish at Hēbōlb did, while the Priest Point village stood unprotected. Since they had no warriors, being a lower class village, they fled to the forest when attacked.

In the summer the people deserted these permanent dwellings and followed the ever changing fishing opportunities and scoured the mountain sides and prairies for roots and berries. If one knew the approximate itinerary of any one group it was possible to guess with fair accuracy where they would be at any given time during the summer, for their wanderings were not altogether undirected.

WINTER HOUSES

The large houses were often from one hundred to two hundred feet long. They were built of cedar planks which were split from the tree trunks with wedges of elk horn. After being split the boards were smoothed with the adze, which was also used in working on canoes. The wall planks were tied to the vertical poles of the framework by means of twisted cedar twigs. Henry, the Nisqually informant, stated that his people always place their wall boards in a horizontal position. He said that other tribes of the neighborhood differ in this respect, the Chehalis, according to him, using vertical boards.[30]

The construction of these houses is well described by Jewitt and by Eells,[31]

---

[28] The Nootka village at Friendly Cove, Vancouver Island, had about twenty houses, that of the "king" being the largest. The smallest was occupied by two families. Jewitt, 65-67.

[29] Lillooet, Teit, (a) 235.

[30] The Twana used both vertical and horizontal boards. Eells, (a) 624.

[31] Jewitt, 65-71.
Eells, (a) 623.

the former using Nootka data and the latter Puget Sound material. The Puget Sound houses were often divided into rooms. The partitions were always built across the width of the house with no opening from one room to the next. Each room had a door to the outside.[32] Small partitions of wood were often built on either side of the door in the interior of the house. These protected the people who lived near the door from the draft.

The doors were both on the long and short sides of the house. A house might have three or four doors. The large winter houses had doors which were closed up by slabs of cedar. The slab operated like the door of a modern house. It swung on an upright pole and was bolted on the inside by means of a horizontal log. This type of door was used in "oldest times"—this is especially verified information.[33] The Nisqually had no swinging doors. A plank of cedar was set in front of the opening.

Around the inside walls of the house was a double row of platforms. The sleeping platforms (xugᵘō′ntɛn) were next to the wall about two and one-half feet from the floor. In front of these were platforms about one foot high, used as seats. Slaves usually slept on these lower platforms if there was no room for them up above. Above the platforms were shelves for storage and they usually slanted toward the wall.

The roof of the old Snohomish houses was the shed type with one pitch (single slope).[34] Doubtless gabled roofs were also used but they were not mentioned. For letting out the smoke the boards in the roof directly above the fireplace were pushed aside.[35]

Henry, the Nisqually informant, knew that the Snohomish used to carve the posts in the houses and he saw carved house posts among the Quinault, but he said the Nisqually never carved their house posts. Sometimes part of the posts were painted red. The house itself was never painted or carved either inside or out.

The walls of the large communal houses were hung with mats. Each person owned the mats that hung in the section where his beds were. Over the beds were the storage shelves and ladders were used to reach them. On them provisions were stored for winter use; no fresh things were ever kept there, only dried provisions such as meat, clams, berries and fish. All these things were stored in baskets. If a person owned any extra blankets they were also stored up there. The floor where people sat was covered with mats and often mats were used as partitions between families in a large house. The fires were arranged around the sides of the house, never in the middle. This space was usually reserved as a passage way from one end of the house to the other. Two to four families had one communal fire. Ordinarily each family ate its meals alone. The

---

[32] Lewis and Clark observed similar divisions inside the houses among the Tillamook, III, 326.

[33] For other types of doors, see Eells, (a) 625.

[34] Gibbs, (a) 215.

[35] Eells, (a) 625 Twana.
BAAS, 1890, 565 Songish.

whole house, however, would gather together for a meal when a hunter or fisherman had been particularly successful.

A large house may be owned by one man or by several of its occupants. Sometimes a whole community would build a potlatch house together, and afterwards would live in it. Some communal houses were partitioned and each room was owned by a family. Even when there were no partitions, each family might own the section of the house they occupied. On the other hand, a chief or a wealthy man might own the entire house, and all the people living in it might be his relatives. In summer they went hunting and fishing together. Among the Nisqually the people who lived on opposite sides of a house usually belonged to one family and had a common fireplace, but each family ate its meals alone.

The owner of the house had the exclusive right to carve his guardian spirit on the house post. The opposite posts were usually carved with the spirit of the same man. When a new owner was taken in at a communal house and there were no house posts left uncarved, he would build a new section onto the old building and carve those posts with his sklaletut. When his carvings were on the new house posts he was regarded as a part owner of the house.

Living houses were inherited by the son from the father. It was not necessary for the son to have any special guardian spirit to inherit the house. If a man had several children, both sons and daughters, then the house belonged to them jointly. If the owner of a house died and left a wife and a son they owned the house jointly.

If an owner died inside the house it was either burnt or given away. In the latter case all people living in the house prior to this person's death had to move out. If a person died in a house which he did not own, the house was not burnt but deserted for a while, about a month or two, and then the occupants would return. A person about to die was not taken out of the house in order that he might die outside.

Each village as far as possible had a potlatch house. Some were also used as ordinary dwelling houses, but wherever the people could afford it they had a special house. The real potlatch house had no partitions inside, but sometimes partitioned houses had to be used. The potlatch house on Guemes Island had partitions, and when the people from different tribes were invited each tribe stayed in a room by itself. This house, according to Shelton, was about two hundred fifty feet long. It was built on a narrow sand bar and was curved a little to follow the bar. It was about thirty-five feet wide. When Shelton saw the house about twenty-two years ago (1917) it was full of people.

The largest potlatch house of the Snohomish was at Tulalip. It was one hundred fifteen feet long and forty-three feet wide. Along the sides were five pairs of semi-cylindrical carved columns[36] on which rested five heavy cross beams. The round side of the columns faced the middle of the house. The columns stood about one yard from the walls. A continuous line of beds ran around the walls. The beds were about four feet wide and covered with mats. The fires were near

---

[36] Rectangular uprights are used by the Songish. BAAS, 1890, 563.

the beds and not in the center of the house. The various families might partition off their sections with mats to protect themselves from cold winds. These mats did not reach to the ceiling but were about six to eight feet high. Sometimes a family placed these mats around their beds and fire leaving just a little passage-way opening into the large room. This house had one door at each end. The walls were made of planks and the roof had a single pitch. Some roof planks were loose so that they could be pushed aside to let the smoke escape.

Another potlatch house was forty-five feet wide and seventy-eight feet long. It had six posts on each of the long sides. These posts were notched at the top so that the transverse beams fitted snugly in the hollow.[37] Every pair of posts except those nearest the doors at opposite ends of the house supported a cross beam. The four posts at the center of the house, two on each side, had figures painted on them in red. Down the middle of the house were three posts, one at each door and one in the center, which supported the ridge pole. These posts were also notched to fit the pole. All the columns except the center one were semi-circular. The center post was round, about two feet in diameter and about twenty-four feet high. Beds were arranged along the long walls and in front of the painted posts. In the newer potlatch houses the decorated columns are on the outer side of the bed platform. The walls were covered with mats up to two feet from the eaves.

SUMMER HOUSES

In the summer time the people migrated from the permanent villages to hunt, fish and gather berries. During this period they lived in temporary summer houses. The Nisqually summer house was either tipi shaped or square. The tipis had a frame of poles tied together at the top and covered with mats which ran horizontally around the structure. The square house had a gabled roof or was a lean-to with a single pitch roof. This frame was also covered with mats and a loose mat at the front served as a door. The fire was always outside. The Nisqually also built temporary houses of brush when camping in the mountains. These were like the square houses and were covered with maple, alder or fir boughs.

The Snuqualmi built a different type of summer house. Four poles forked at the upper end were set in the ground to make the four corners of the house. On these rested the horizontal poles which supported a gabled roof. The frame-work of the house was tied together with cedar twigs (stĕdgwad). The roof and three of the sides were covered with mats (K!wā'daq). The front was com-pletely open, but when it rained a mat was hung down from the roof and served as a door. The front of the house faced the fire which was built just outside.[38] Several families built their mat houses around a common fire, and all houses faced this central spot. When people went out camping they took all the parts of the

---

[37] BAAS, 1890, 563. Songish.
[38] Eells states that the fire of the summer lodge was inside, in the center. Eells, (a) 625.

house with them so that it could be erected quickly. The mats were tied to the frame by means of the twisted inside blades of dried cattail rushes.

The Snohomish never made the tipi-like summer house. This type was characteristic of the Klikitat and Nisqually. The summer house of the Snohomish was similar to the square house of the Nisqually. The mats were arranged in tiers and overlapped at the edges so that they would shed rain. If several families occupied one house it would sometimes be as much as thirty feet long. Usually they were much smaller and were used by one family alone. This type of summer house was called g.ᵘElai'txᵘ. Ordinarily the mats extended down to the ground, but occasionally vertical boards were built up for the sides and mats used only for the roof. This type of house was not found frequently.

ECONOMIC LIFE

VARIETIES AND PREPARATION OF FOOD

The tribes of this area subsisted principally on roots, berries, fish and meat. The chief tribal differences in regard to food were the proportion of seafood to meat. For instance, the Nisqually who lived on the Sound had large quantities of clams, while those of the interior only secured them occasionally through trading camas and dried meat for seafood. The Snohomish lived principally on seafood and, in contrast to the Snuqualmi, did little hunting. The Snuqualmi were the best hunters of the Puget Sound tribes[39] and went far into the mountains on snowshoes in pursuit of game. There was much trading in food as well as in other things between the Snohomish and the Snuqualmi. The Skagit carried this even further. They also were good hunters and after drying large quantities of meat, they would load it on canoes and travel down the Sound, trading their stores of meat for other supplies.

Every kind of food used by these tribes was a spontaneous product of nature, and its gathering continued practically throughout the year. Although the people had permanent winter houses, they moved about a great deal in order to be near to the particular kind of food they were collecting at the time.[40] In May the people left their winter houses to get clams and other kinds of shell fish. When a large supply was obtained and dried they took them back to the winter house. Then they set out again, the women to gather roots and berries, the men to hunt. Again the supplies were taken to winter quarters, and then the most important pursuit of the year, namely fishing, began. The fishing season lasted until the beginning of November. When that was over, the people returned to their winter houses for the season. During the winter, small parties would go out for seal or ducks, the latter being caught by torchlight during this season. The Snohomish hunted seal both in winter and summer, while the Nisqually and Snuqualmi rarely went after seal at all.

All vegetable foods were gathered and prepared by the women. Roots were dug with a digging stick about two and one-half feet long, usually made of the wood of some conifer. The women went to the open prairie for roots, to the mountains for berries and around the lakes for the wild potato. The roots of the brake fern (Pteridium aquilinum) and the wood fern (Dryopteris dilatata) were gathered in fall and winter whenever the plant was not growing, and used as food.[41] Other roots were those of the dandelion and a wild species of sunflower. The big roots of the cattail (ōlɛl) were considered a delicacy and were eaten raw. Bulbs of plants were also used in great quantities. The most important in this area was the camas (sxa'zɛb), which was dug on Nisqually prairie. The bulb of

---

[39] Gibbs, (a), 193.
[40] Gibbs, (a), 197.
[41] Dr. T. C. Frye of the University of Washington was kind enough to identify these plants from specimens collected by Dr. Haeberlin.

the tiger lily (Lilium parviflorum Holzinger)[42] (tsa'gwitc) was steamed in a pit and eaten. Another important food product among the bulbous plants were the various kinds of so-called potatoes. One of the most widespread species is "wappato,"[43] which grows in shallow lakes and creeks, or any land flooded by fresh water. The bulb is the size of an egg, has white meat and is very sweet and nutritious. This plant can easily be grown and transplanted.[44] Wapato Lake and Wapato Creek were especially good areas for its growth. Another species of potato is called sxaasEm; it is like the ordinary potato only very much smaller.

A large variety of berries were used. They were: salmonberry, huckleberry, blackberry (gudbi'x̱u), raspberry, salalberry (t!a'qa'), serviceberry, wild strawberry, and blackcaps. These berries were eaten fresh or dried. The wild carrot (cāgaq) was eaten raw or boiled. Acorns were more important for some Puget Sound people, as for instance the Nisqually, than for others, but everyone seems to have made some use of them. Hazelnuts were also gathered.

The meat of the elk, deer, beaver, mountain-goat, wild-cat, bear, groundhog (cauɬ), cougar, several varieties of ducks, grouse and pheasants (sq^ulōb) was eaten. These animals were shot or snared. It was especially pointed out that they never ate eagles, gulls,[45] or hawks.

There was greater variety in fish. Five kinds of salmon were caught; they were in the order of the salmon runs: spring (yo'batc), humpback (ha'do'), silver (skwa'x̱wits), dog (L!xwai'), and steelhead (skwa'wu'l). The spring salmon was most desirable. Small fish like smelts, herring, flounders, trout were caught in abundance. Smelts and herring were prized for their richness in oil and were dried in large quantities. The Snohomish caught sturgeon, while they and the other coast people used cod, rock cod and skates. Several kinds of shell fish were used such as: clams, oysters, barnacles and crabs. When constantly picked, barnacles became large and juicy and were preferred to the oyster. Only certain places where the beach was clean and the tide ran swiftly were visited for barnacles, for those in sluggish water frequently were poisonous. Both fish and bird eggs were eaten; of the latter, pheasant, lark[46] and duck were most common, of the former, salmon eggs. Seal grease was used with food, but it was not as important in diet as grease and fish oil are further to the north.

Deer and elk meat were considered best varieties and dried with special care. The meat was cut in pieces and hung on a frame. Fires were built on three sides and the meat was thoroughly roasted. Then it was hung higher to dry more slowly. When done in this way, the meat would keep a long time. Hunters often dried meat in the mountains and cached it in trees, covering it with boughs and mats to keep it dry. It was afterwards collected or eaten by other hunters. In the house

---

[42] Frye and Rigg.
[43] Swan states that the wappato is the bulb of the common Saggita Folia or arrowhead. Swan. (a) 90.
[44] This is the only reference of any kind of cultivation. In 1854 the Sound Indians are supposed to have raised 11,000 bushels of potatoes. The species is not stated. These may have been ordinary potatoes, Indian potatoes or wappato. Gibbs, (a) 197.
[45] Gulls were occasionally eaten by old people among the Twana. Eells, (a) 619.
[46] Lark's eggs boiled were given to little children to make them good talkers.

dried meat was stored in baskets, never in a hole. In winter it was soaked in water and boiled. Ground hog, wildcat, cougar, beaver, and mountain goat meat was never dried.

The tribes on the Sound used seal oil (xᵘtsa′q!ᵘ), which was kept in seal bladders (xadzo′b) and fish bladders. Seal grease was eaten with dried salmon and clams. Often seal oil was poured on the fire to make it burn better. The Snuqualmi did not use any seal oil because they lived too far inland. They used instead deer and elk fat, which was dried and stored in large baskets that were hung in the house. This dried fat was eaten with other foods.

Salmon were dried or smoked. Near the winter houses there were sometimes little outsheds used for smoking salmon: some of these huts had a gabled roof and others were a simple lean-to. Salmon was prepared for drying or for immediate use by cutting it open on the dorsal side; the head and tail were cut off, but the skin was left on. After splitting, the backbone was taken out and the entrails were given to the dogs. The pieces of fish were fastened to sticks and stretched out by means of cross-sticks. Salmon was smoked over a fire in the house or shed. When the salmon was used at once it was roasted on a stick stuck in the ground and leaning toward the fire. The backbone was dried over the fire and sucked. The head was also eaten. Dried salmon was called K!aṇa′ṇa′. Flounders were not dried because they would not keep.

Before butchering a seal it was rolled over in the fire until the hair was singed off. Then the skin was scraped.[47] The seal was cut open on the dorsal side and the fat taken off. Then a ventral incision was made and the entrails were removed.[48]

Berries such as salmon, service, red and black huckleberries, wild strawberries, elder, salal, blackcaps, blackberries and wild raspberries were usually sun dried for winter use. Often they were dried over the fire, spread on cedar bark. Another way of preserving berries was to mash them in a large basket and then mold them into cakes.[49] Blackberries were mashed and mixed with blackcaps and sun dried or dried by the fire. Then they were molded into round forms about two inches thick called tuckams and could be kept indefinitely. Salal and huckleberries were prepared in the same way. Soup was made of these dried berries in winter.

A great deal of food was cached for future use, not only by travellers, but also near the permanent villages. Meat was always put in the trees and covered with cedar bark to keep out the rain. Hazel nuts with the shells on were cached in the ground but after the shells had been removed they were put in trees. These nuts were never cooked. Acorns were generally cooked before caching. After the acorns were boiled the Nisqually put them in an openwork basket and buried them in the mud of the lake. The acorns had to be completely covered with mud and water. This method was used only after the acorns had been cooked. When they were taken out of the water they were not boiled again but only soaked before

---

[47] This is also done by the Kwakiutl. Boas, (a) 451; Swan, (a) 83.
[48] The Kwakiutl used a different method of butchering. Boas, (a) 453.
[49] Eells, (a) 622.

eating. Just as the hazel nuts were buried in the ground before the shells were removed, so the acorns were also cached in this fashion. The shells came off very easily when the nuts were unearthed. When the Nisqually travelled they cached camas in trees, never in the ground. The camas were cooked, dried, put in baskets lined with maple leaves and set in the trees.

The principal methods of cooking were boiling with hot stones, steaming in a pit and roasting by an open fire.[50] Ordinary stone boiling, called sk"alts, was used for many kinds of food and was done in water-tight coiled baskets. The pits for cooking were always outdoors and often as much as four to five feet deep. After the food was placed in a pit in which there had been a fire, it was covered with boughs and earth and a fire again started on top. Fish, meat and certain kinds of bulbs were cooked in this manner. The following are some specific recipes: SpE'nEm: after the pit in the sand had been heated, the fire was removed and the pit filled with potatoes and covered with hot sand. Fish roasted in this manner were wrapped in maple leaves.[51] SL!a'Ls: stones were heated in a fire of cedar wood and on these fish, meat or clams were laid and covered with mats. Seal meat was cooked in this way, but that was always cut into small pieces. Camas were cooked in essentially the same way. The pit was covered with earth and a fire built on top. It took from two to four days, according to the quantity of bulbs. When dried in the sun after being cooked, camas kept from one season to another. Dried camas soaked in water made excellent soup.

Meat was fried, boiled or roasted, each kind of meat always being prepared by one particular process. Boiling was usually done in water-tight baskets, but when large quantities were prepared at once it was often put in a canoe filled with water and hot stones. Meat was also roasted like camas. Deer meat seems to be the only kind that was ever fried. This was done by wrapping the meat with some grease in a strip of cedar bark and putting it over hot stones. Ducks were usually boiled in baskets but sometimes were roasted on a spit over the fire. Groundhog, cougar, wildcat, beaver, and mountain goat were roasted, never fried or boiled. Bear, deer, and elk meat was dried and then roasted.

One of the most popular ways of preparing fish was to roast it on a stick over the fire. This method was called sk!e'Em. A stick about two feet long was split in half to about three-fourths of its length. The fish was split on one side and stuck lengthwise into the split stick. Then the stick was tied together just above and below the fish so as to keep the fish in a fixed position. Little sticks were inserted in a crosswise position in order to keep the fish flat so that the heat could get at the whole piece. The long stick was stuck into the ground in a slanting position and a fire was built under it. Salmon was split and roasted in the same way. This was called sq!ᵘo'lEm. Large clams were also roasted in this fashion, and after roasting they were strung on cedar bark and hung up for winter use. To bake clams they were stuck on sticks, seven large ones to one stick. Two forked sticks were set upon the beach about six feet apart and a horizontal

---

[50] Compare this section generally with Klallam cooking methods. Gunther, 209.
[51] Used by the Twana. Eells, (a) 618.

stick laid on them. This supported the slanting sticks with the clams. The lower ends of these sticks rested on a board. Underneath the slanting sticks a fire was built with a log rolled on each side to concentrate the heat. When the clams at the lower end were well roasted the stick was turned. Clams, oyster, mussels and barnacles were smoked and strung on buckskin or sticks for winter use. None of these were eaten raw. They were often steamed on hot rocks, covered with mats.

Acorns, fern roots and sprouts of salmon berries were eaten with salmon eggs, but hazel nuts were never eaten with salmon eggs. Salmon was often boiled with camas. Sallal berries and tiger lily bulbs were eaten with salmon eggs, but huckleberries, blackberries or raspberries were not. The bark of fern roots was served with dried salmon eggs.

Tea[52] (Lɛexō'lsā'led) was made from dried huckleberry leaves. The root of the wild sunflower was soaked in cold water for several hours, giving a very desirable drink.

Only two meals a day were served; the first about nine o'clock in the morning and the second a little before six at night.[53]

When soup was boiled in a basket with hot stones, the stones were left in the basket when it was served. When the basket was nearly empty the stones were removed and the basket was scraped out with the fingers.

The Snohomish used shells (tc!au'wa'i) as spoons both to eat with and to dip the food out of the baskets. Among the Nisqually each person had his own plate. At a general feast the girls and women served but often the men helped.[54]

After the death of a relative a person was only permitted to eat meat and fish which had been dried for at least six weeks. This regulation did not apply to vegetable foods.

If several sturgeon or seals were caught, the successful hunters invited their friends and gave a feast. Each guest received a piece of sturgeon or seal to take home.

FIRE MAKING

Fire was made with the usual hand drill, each locality using a particular kind of wood for the instruments. One set had a hearth of cottonwood root and a drill of cedar, both very dry. The hearth had the usual series of notches on one side. Tinder of fine shredded cedar bark was placed directly at the notches. The twirling of the cedar drill caused the shredded bark to ignite.

Another instrument called cō'laᴋtcup was made of the roots of the xā"q!tī a tree which grows along the upper part of the Snohomish River, only the hearth and the drill being black wild cherry. The point of the drill was bound to the

[52] The Twana used hemlock leaves for tea. Eells, (a) 618.
[53] Klallam, Gunther, 210.
[54] Klallam, Gunther, 211.

shaft by means of wild cherry bark.[55] If the roots of the xā"q!tī could not be obtained then pussy willow was used for the point of the drill and the hearth. Again very dry cedar bark was used as tinder.

The Nisqually set up fire with bark. When travelling, they had a slow torch (pᴇdā'q) which was a piece of shredded cedar bark about four feet long, wrapped in unshredded cedar bark. One end was kept burning and in this way fire could be carried for several days.[56]

HUNTING

The people of this area were interested in both land and sea hunting, the Skykomish, Snuqualmi and Skagit being concerned more with the former. These tribes living farther inland, hunted deer, elk, bear, mountain-goat and smaller animals like beaver and groundhog. Elk were run down and killed when exhausted.[57] The hunters believed that elk always return in a large circle to the place where they started, since they want to come home to die.

A trap for bears consisted of two poles about ten feet high erected over some bear tracks. These carried a heavy horizontal pole to which a rope was attached. This rope was also tied to brush that covered up a four to five foot hole dug underneath the horizontal pole. When the bear stepped on the brush and fell into the hole, he pulled down the horizontal pole which fell on him.[58]

Beaver were speared when hunters in canoes broke their dam open. The spear had a shaft of fir about two feet long with a foreshaft of deer bone and a barbed point also of bone. Beaver hunting was done by daylight.

Seal hunting, practiced by the lower Sound groups but never by the Nisqually, was done from canoes with a two pronged harpoon, the shaft of which was about twelve feet long. When the weapon was thrown, the two points pierced the animal and it was held in tow by the line attached to them but independent of the shaft. Sturgeon was taken in the same way.

Ducks were hunted in various ways. Hell divers were taken at night with a six pronged spear. Each prong had from one to five barbs. A long rope was attached to the shaft. This weapon was used from the prow of a canoe with a paddler in the stern directly in front of a fire of pitchwood which attracted the birds. Ducks, especially mallards, were also taken at night with a large net six feet long, stretched between two poles that were fastened to a crosspole held by the hunter. He stood in the prow of a canoe with a pitch fire and a paddler in the stern. The canoe ran into a flock of ducks and the hunter plunged the net down on them. The Snohomish used a large duck net like the tukum of the

---

[55] The spliced drill is a common feature among the Great Basin tribes, but the only instance, except the one cited here, recorded outside of that area is among the Klamath. Lowie, (a) 189. Hough, (a) 536, 538-539.

[56] The Klallam carried embers in a clam shell. Gunther, 211.

[57] The Lillooet did this in the fall when the bucks were fat and short winded. Teit. (a) 226.

[58] Lillooet, Teit, (a) 226; Thompson, Teit, (b) 249.

Klallam.[59] These nets (tuku'b) were hung between two tall, lone-standing trees. One such net was placed near Snuqualmi Jim's house on Mission Beach to catch ducks and geese as they flew out from the bay.

There were two kinds of arrows, one for hunting and another for war.[60] Stone arrowheads were buried in a fire to harden them. Frequently they were poisoned with a medicine that made the flesh of an animal swell.[61]

The Nisqually informant emphatically denied the use of poisoned arrows. The shaft was feathered with duck feathers, fastened with deer sinew (tĕ'dc).

Quivers (tcEla'x^u) were made of wildcat, coonskin, and wolfskin, with the hair on the outside. The skin was sewn together at the ends and laced on one side with buckskin from the top to about three-fourths of its length. The remainder was left open to take out the arrows. A quiver was usually about two and three-quarters feet long and the arrows were two and one-half feet. The open part of the quiver was toward the front in carrying. Quivers were always carried on the left side and fastened with a buckskin strap.

Bows were made of yewwood.[62] For shooting, the thumb and little finger were on the side of the bow facing the marksman. The forefinger and middle finger were erect and the arrow was shot between these two fingers.

A club for killing fish (K!ōXu'stEdad) was made of maple or alder.

Slings for killing birds (ła'łEmt) were about three feet long, made of willow bark string. The pocket for the missile was made of a small piece of skin. The string had loops at the ends for the fingers.

When a man is hunting he sings his spirit songs. If he hears his spirit singing he knows he will be successful. A man can kill the animal whose spirit he has, because he has only the spirit, which has no connection with the real animal. A hunter must avoid people who have been in contact with a dead body. The wife of a hunter must not break open bones to extract the marrow while her husband is out hunting, lest he fall and break his legs. Nor may a hunter's wife give a dog the meat of any animal her husband shot; if she did, the wild animals would kill him.

FISHING

Although the Sound people did not depend wholly on fishing as a means of subsistence, still it was a very important means of obtaining food. The fishing season began in midsummer and continued until the beginning of November. During this period the people usually left their winter houses and camped along the rivers by the fishing grounds. The first salmon caught in a season was treated with great ceremony so that the fishing might be successful.[63]

[59] Gunther, 205.
[60] The Thompson poisoned arrows with the juice of the flowers of Ranunculus sp. or with rattlesnake poison. Teit, (b) 243.
[61] Thompson, Teit, (b) 243.
[62] The lower Thompson used yewwood, dogwood and hemlock. Teit, (b) 239.
[63] For a discussion of this ceremony, see Gunther, (b).

Salmon fishing[64] was done by means of nets, traps, or weirs, fishing with hook and line or trailing a net.[65] Salmon were also speared like seal and sturgeon.

A salmon weir described by Snuqualmi Jim was used as follows: Several sets of alder wood poles (Figure II), were set up in tripod fashion across a

Fig. II. Salmon Trap.

river or creek where the water was quite shallow. The whole stream was fenced off with willow staves about 8 feet long and one to two inches thick, stuck side by side in the river bed and lashed together with string. The row of willow sticks was fastened to the tripods, which were held together by a long pole. The water came about to half the height of the willow sticks. Each tripod had a platform above the water which was about 6 feet square. The fisherman stood on this, holding a long pole with a dip net about 4 or 5 feet long at the end. In coming up the river the salmon were held back by the fence and the water at the trap would be full of fish. The men on the platforms took the salmon out of the water with their dip nets and clubbed them to death.

The Indians had such weirs near their summer camping place. It took a great deal of labor to construct them. Unless the water was thick and dirty, they got salmon at night. Such a weir was called stEqa'lEk[u]. Shelton explained stEq means closed and -alEk[u] is evidently the suffix for water.[66]

When the salmon first began to run they were caught in salt water. The men went out in a canoe, the forward man paddling, the man in the stern trailing a line and hook.[67] The hook was of bone and baited with a clam.[68] When the line was not used it was wrapped on a little board called tētκ!obā'lo'.

---

[64] A good description of Chinook methods of salmon fishing is given in Swan, (a) 104.

[65] Thompson. Teit, (b) 250.

[66] This type of weir used also by the Yakima. Gibbs, (b) 407.

[67] A hook and line method is described for the Shoalwater Bay Indians by Swan, (a) 137.

[68] Swan states that the Indians never attempted to catch salmon with a baited hook. The hook was used as a "gaff." Swan, (a) 264.

Salmon were also caught in salt water by means of a long net made of nettle string.[69] The rope to which the net was attached was made of willow twigs. Stones were tied to one side of the net to weight it and floats were attached to the other.

The Nisqually constructed a salmon trap across narrow streams which consisted of two fences made of fir staves fastened with cedar twigs. The fences were held in place by horizontal logs. The upstream fence slanting to the right was solid, while the downstream fence, slanting to the left, had an opening of about two feet to allow the salmon to gather between the two fences. Platforms were built across the stream on which the fishermen stood with dip nets.

Another device for catching salmon was a large cylindrical net (ca'bEd) which was fastened to two cedar poles that were held by men in canoes. They moved downstream, dragging the net so that the water kept it open. A smaller net of this type was used for trout. When the salmon were coming upstream, four men went out, in two canoes, one at the bow and one at the stern of each. The man in the stern held a funnel shaped net in the water by means of poles. The poles were held vertically in the water. From the bow of each canoe, a string on which small pieces of white willow bark were fastened ran to the net. The fish would see these and follow them into the net. When there was moonlight no fire was used, but on dark nights a fire of pitchwood was built in the middle of each canoe. This method of fishing was also used for trout, in which case the meshes of the net were smaller.

Trout in the rivers were often caught with hook and line, salmon eggs being the usual bait.[70]

There were several ways of catching flounders. A net (lē'ᴋ!ᵘdjō) about two hundred feet wide and ten feet high was suspended in shallow water by means of stone sinkers and cedar bark floats. The meshes of the net, made of nettle string, were measured with a maple wood gauge (t!a'ɫotcid). The fisherman in a canoe beat the water with a hard wood club (po'xᵘtid) to drive the fish into the net, which was then doubled up and pulled in. The Nisqually caught flounders by setting up a line to which strings with hooks baited with worms were attached. Each hook consisted of two pointed pieces of bone tied together so that the points faced in opposite directions. The Snohomish speared flounders at night by pitch fires. The Snuqualmi never caught flounders.

Smelts and herring were taken at night with a rake of cedar (ɫa'tabEd). This was about twelve inches long with pointed pegs of ironwood. The fish are tossed over the fisherman's shoulder into the canoe with this.

Seal and sturgeon[71] were usually pursued with a harpoon (taɫ) with detachable point. The harpoon shaft was made of fir, the foreshaft of yew and the prongs of ironwood. The point was of yewwood or bone, and the rope of twisted cedar. A float shaped like a duck was made of cedar bark and attached

---

[69] BAAS 1890, 567—preparation of nettle bark for netting.

[70] The Chinook use salmon roe. Swan, (a) 189.

[71] The Chinook of Baker's Bay catch sturgeon by means of a salmon hook attached to a long cod line. They go out in a canoe, feel for the fish, stick the hook into it and after it is exhausted, kill it by clubbing and haul it into the canoe. Swan, (a) 245.

to the line that was fastened to the harpoon point to indicate the position of the animal. The rope was fastened to the shaft with a slip knot which opened when the harpoon was thrown. The float was always made by a person having a tc!ā'dyo' spirit.

MONEY AND MONEY VALUES

In trading both along the coast and with the interior tribes, shell money was used. As shell money travelled eastward over the mountains it became more valuable. There were several kinds of shell money. tc!au'wai were discs of clam shell about one centimeter in diameter. The shell must be white. A hole was made in each bead so that it could be strung and the disc was smoothed with a rough stone. These clam shells were found in the Snohomish country. tc!au'wai was always strung in single strings. Solax was made from the shells traded in from the north. It had the form of tubular beads, strung in pairs with a round bead between. Solax was always measured double, so although the Indians claimed it to be only half as valuable as tc!au'wai, it was equal in value, bead for bead, for two lengths of tc!au'wai were equal to one of solax. Single shells in the string must not be broken, for that diminished the total value of the piece. xᵘtciɫqs was made of the shell of a very large clam found in the north. Since it was not found in the Snohomish territory, it was highly prized by them. Two to four large shells were worth a slave. Pieces of this money were worn at the end of a necklace, or a chief would have a piece in each ear. A Snohomish informant said that he had never heard of dentalium money.

VALUES AND MEASUREMENTS

One-half fathom (muxᵘnɛgᵘe'ngᵘas)=distance from middle of breast to end of thumb, arm stretched out.

One fathom (nɛntcax'ᵘtaɫ)=from fingers of one hand to fingers of the other, arms outstretched.

20 fathoms of solax money=one slave (if all the shells were good).

30-40 fathoms of solax money=one very good slave.

2-4 large shells of expensive northern money=one slave.

8 fathoms of tc!au'wai=one good canoe (not the largest kind).

4 fathoms of solax=one canoe.

1 fathom of solax=one basket.

2 fathoms of solas=one very good basket.

One slave boy=20 groundhog skins or one blanket of groundhog, or five otter skins, or two beaver skins, or one bear skin or five undressed deer skins or one dressed deer skin.

One slave, man or woman in prime of life=60 groundhog skins or three blankets of groundhog, or ten otter skins, or five beaver skins, or two bear skins and one beaver skin, or ten undressed deer skins, or two dressed deer skins.[72]

---

[72] One slave is worth one large net for catching salmon. One good slave is worth ten fathoms of dentalium, two dressed buck skins and one dressed elk skin. One slave of less value is worth from five double fathoms of dentalium to five double fathoms of dentalium and one canoe. Thompson, Teit, (b) 261.

CRAFTS

The following notes on the crafts of the Snohomish and Snuqualmi Indians are very fragmentary. These arts disappeared rapidly after contact with the whites, and the following accounts are given largely by people who no longer practice them. There was no predominating industry as the wood carving of the northern Indians or the basketry of the Pomo. The articles were made for utilitarian purposes and were not outstanding from either the technical or aesthetic point of view.

WEAVING

The Snohomish, Skykomish and Snuqualmi shared with the Klallam and Cowichans the use of woven blankets of mountain goat wool, dog hair or a combination of feathers and fireweed. The Snohomish did not hunt the mountain goat but bought the wool from the Skykomish. They also raised dogs (sqē'xa) exclusively for their wool, as did the Klallam.[73] For shearing, the dogs' forelegs were tied together and the wool was cut with a stone knife. The wool was sometimes dyed pink with hemlock or alder bark. The Snuqualmi, Skykomish and Nisqually did not have these dogs.

Blankets (sta'tek!ᵘ) were made of the soft down duck feathers, stripped from the quills and pounded with a hardwood stick. Then they were mixed with the downy fibres of the giant fireweed (*epilobium angustifolium*)[74] (xa'tc!t). This mixture was spun into thread by twisting on the thigh and this thread was used as the weft of the blanket. The warp was made of nettle bark. The blanket was woven on the same loom as the mountain-goat wool blanket and closely resembled the finished product, except that it was darker in color. The Snuqualmi and Skykomish did not make this type of blanket and the Nisqually learned it only recently.

The mountain-goat wool blanket is still being woven on Vancouver Island, but few Indians of Puget Sound today have ever made them or seen them made. Mrs. William Bagley, a Snuqualmi on the Tulalip Reservation, saw her mother weave these blankets and in her girlhood learned the technique herself.[75] The Snohomish informant of Dr. Haeberlin describes the processing of spinning as follows:

Wool was carded with the fingers until American wool cards were introduced.[76] The wool was twisted on the right thigh, first into a single strand in one direction, then doubled and twisted in the opposite direction. It seems that the direction in which the single strand was twisted was not uniform, for this informant said she always worked away from the hip, while others twisted it toward the hip.[77]

---

[73] Gunther, 221.
[74] Identified by Dr. T. C. Frye.
[75] Fuller notes on weaving were secured by Miss Mary Davis and will be published in a discussion of local weaving by Dr. Leslie Spier.
[76] Preparation of wool before spinning, Teit, (a) 211.
[77] Same method used for fibers by the Chinook and Clatsop. Swan, (a) 163.

The spinning was done with a spindle and whorl. The twisted thread was wound on the spindle near the whorl and the spindle was set into motion by twisting one end of it on the right thigh. The other end was held up high by means of the thread held in the left hand and further twisted by the rotation of the spindle. When part of the thread was spun sufficiently, it was wound on the spindle. Then while the spinner twisted more wool on her thigh, she held the spindle under the knee.

The loom for this weaving consisted of two upright posts each with two holes cut about five feet apart to receive the ends of the horizontal rollers. Generally the men made these looms, which in the Puget Sound country were simple, but farther north were often nicely carved.[78] The uprights were set in the ground either indoors or out. In the north the looms were so tall that a scaffold had to be erected for the weaver. A loom string is tied to the uprights parallel to the roller and close to it. The first warp is fastened to this, run behind and over the upper roller, down on the front, under the lower roller and up to the string, over which it is passed before it is put over the upper roller again (see Fig. III). The blanket is begun at the upper left corner, the weft being put in with the fingers. The first row is twined with a piece of yarn just long enough for the row with a loop finish at the right side. In the second row the twilling, of which the remainder of the blanket is woven,

Fig. III. Roller Loom for Salish Mountain Goat Blanket.

is begun. The weft is loosely put in so that it shows equally with the warp. The work is moved to the back as it is finished. When the blanket is completed the loom string is drawn, opening the piece to its full length.

These blankets are used as bedding and as occasional clothing, their weight being too great for constant use.

---

[78] Description of loom, Gibbs, (a) 220; Songish, Boas, BAAS 1890, 567.

CEDAR BARK SHREDDING[79]

Cedar bark for shredding is gathered when the sap is running. The inner bark of the tree is torn off in long strips and stored away until it is softened or shredded for use. This is accomplished by laying the bark over the edge of a paddle, that rests in the fork of a stick, stuck in the ground, and chopping it with a flat chopper of maple wood. This chopper resembles a mincing knife in operation and somewhat in shape. It is about six inches long and four inches tall, with a hole near the top large enough for the hand to grasp it. Bark may be coarsely or finely shredded according to its proposed use.

MATS[80]

The Nisqually women used cedar bark and cat tail rushes[81] for weaving mats (kŏt).[82] The cattail mats were made by running nettle string through the rushes with a long, slightly curved needle that was triangular in cross section. While the needle was still in the mat a creaser (xadā'lōsīd) was run over it so that a ridge was formed on the outside. Then the string was pulled through the length of the needle. The length of the rushes formed the width of the mat. The ends were braided in with strips of cat tail rush.

The mats were used as mattresses, as wall hangings and for covers for the temporary summer houses.[83] Smaller mats were used by fishermen to kneel on in the canoe, and to tie about their shoulders to shed water.

BASKETRY

Since the original publication of this paper, the extensive monograph by Haeberlin, Teit and Roberts on "Salish Basketry"[84] has appeared, making these notes seem very fragmentary. They are included for the sake of completeness, but the other paper should be consulted for an adequate description of the basketry.

There were tribal differences in the kinds of baskets woven, but through trading it seemed that every tribe secured some examples of each type. Coiled baskets were made by the Snuqualmi and Nisqually, the latter supposedly having taught the Klikitat the technique. The Snohomish made no coiled baskets, but they, and even to a greater extent, the Skykomish, made soft twined baskets with borders of dog wool. The Nisqually also made loosely twined baskets[85] with twilled bottoms, but never closely twined baskets. The Snohomish, Snuqualmi and Skykomish all made twined baskets. The Snohomish, Snuqualmi and Nisqually made small basketry caps worn only by the women.

---

[79] For further detail and uses among the Klallam, see Gunther, 219.

[80] Gunther, 220.

[81] The preparation of cattails for matting is described by Swan, (a) 161.

[82] The Thompson and Lillooet use tule rushes for mats. Teit, (a) 208.

[83] Interior tribes like the Lillooet used bark and brush on summer shelters instead of mats. Teit, (a) 215.

[84] Haeberlin, Teit, and Roberts, "Salish Basketry" RBAE, 41.

[85] Perhaps the open work and crossed warp twined is meant by this.

The foundation of the coiled basket was made of dried cedar roots (ts!apx).[86] The material for black imbrication was the root of the horsetail (*Equisitum telmaleia*) (dlā'bts). The material for white imprication was bear grass or Indian grass (*Xerophyllum tenax*) (tcatō'lbixᵘ), which grows in the Cascades and around Mt. Rainier about 500 to 1500 feet below the snow line during the summer. This was also used as the overlay strip in twined baskets. The red imbrication was done with cedar root, and wild cherry was used for brown. These materials were all dried and stored until used. Then they were soaked in water to make them pliable. The Snuqualmi used a sharp bone awl for making basketry. When a twined basket (xalā'n.otsid) was finished, it was filled with dry sand and leaves and allowed to stand a few hours to straighten it out. Carrying straps were braided of maple bark and overlaid with bear grass.

Soft baskets (gᵘɛso'mos) were used by the Snohomish for storing things in the house. They were never taken out for berrying or gathering roots. Coiled baskets were made especially for cooking purposes. The loosely twined baskets were used by the Nisqually for storing dried foods. Often these baskets were lined with maple leaves.[87]

SKINWORK

Deer skin was the only hide which the Snohomish tanned on both sides. Groundhog, beaver, otter, and bear were all used with the hair on.

Deerskin was soaked in water for three days. Then it was hung over an upright pole about six inches in diameter, and scraped with a deer rib. First the inside was cleaned and then the hair was scraped off the outside. Deer brains were dried over the fire and soaked in warm water. The skin was immersed in this liquid and left to soak for three days. When it was taken out, it was rinsed and then wrung between two sticks. One of these sticks was attached to each end of the skin and they were twisted. When the skin was dry it was rubbed with a rough stone to make it pliable. Finally it was hung over the fire for about one hour to smoke it.[88]

The Nisqually formerly made parfleches of stiff untanned elk skin from which the hair had been removed. The designs were painted on in red, the same paint that was used for facial painting. The parfleches were used for carrying provisions and also for storing smoked meat and tanned buckskins. The Chehalis and the Indians east of the mountains also used parfleches.

TOOLS

Trees were felled with wedges (gwa'daкᵘ) of elk horn[89] or yew wood. The wedge was about one foot long and made in one piece. In felling a tree a groove was chipped around the trunk and the wedges driven in with a stone maul

---

[86] The Lillooet used finely split cedar roots for the foundation of their finest baskets. Teit, (a) 205.
[87] Compare with Klallam. Gunther, 222.
[88] Gunther, 219.
[89] Thompson, Teit, (b) 182.

(sĸā'tcīd). The mauls and stone spear points were polished by being placed in a fire of white fir needles. Water was poured on the fire which made the pitch ooze from the needles and cover the stone, which was then taken out, dipped in water and polished with another stone. The adzes used in making canoes had blades of white stone. The adze used by the Nisqually had a short handle.[90]

The digging stick of the Nisqually had a handle of elkhorn[91] and a shaft of hardwood. For cutting meat and fish a knife (stō'ᵘĸᵘ) of stone with a yew wood handle was used. The blade was sharp on one edge only.

WOOD WORK

The Puget Sound people represent a very marginal development in the art of wood working, having essentially the forms used to the north, but none of the artistic finish or even fine technical skill. Perhaps the best example of their wood working are their canoes, of which several types were in common use. They were all dugouts made of cedar.[92] The bow and stern of the large canoes of the Snohomish were always made of separate pieces of cedar. . The smaller canoes were made of one piece when a suitable log could be found. The process of widening the sides was the same for all types. Water was put in the canoe and heated with hot stones. A slow fire was built under the canoe. Great care had to be taken not to have the canoe crack from the heat. Thwarts were forced in to spread the sides apart. If a canoe cracked, it was patched with pitch of spruce or fir. The pitch was applied with hot rocks handled by means of tongs. This pitch was kept in clam shells and always taken along for emergencies.

The following types of canoes were used by the Puget Sound tribes:

1. The large canoe (a″ōtxs),[93] which held six to fifteen persons. It was painted black on the outside and red inside.[94] It was never used by the Nisqually. The Snohomish used it for travelling and the Snuqualmi made use of this type when they came to the Sound. This type of canoe was not used by the Snohomish in the early days. Even later they did not make it but bought it from the Neah Bay Indians for shell money and slaves. The type is probably indigenous at Neah Bay.

2. The Quinault canoe[95] was even larger than the one mentioned above. It held about sixty people. It was a dugout with very high bow and stern. This type was rare among the Sound Indians. The Snohomish bought such canoes but never made them.

---

[90] The Quinault used an adze with an elk horn handle. Willoughby, 267.
[91] The Chinook had a digging stick with a horn handle. Bancroft, I, 237.
[92] The Lillooet used bark canoes formerly, but make some dugout canoes now. Teit, (a) 229.
[93] This type is called a war canoe by Waterman. It is known on the Coast and in the Sound as the Chinook model. Waterman, (a) 15.
[94] Bancroft notes this same color scheme as prevalent among the Sound Indians. Bancroft, I, 216.
[95] Waterman states that this type of canoe is used by all tribes from Columbia River to the northern end of Vancouver Island. Waterman, (a) 16.

3.   A light canoe (stiwa'tł)[96] was used by the women especially. The bow and stern were alike. It was painted like the large canoe.

4.   The smallest canoe (sta'x̱wił)[97] was used for hunting ducks and fishing. It was usually made for two people. It was a light, fast boat and very low. The color was the same as that of the larger canoes. The Snohomish and Nisqually used this especially in rivers, although the Nisqually did go on the Sound with it.

5.   The shovel nose canoe (L!ai)[98] was probably the most common type. The Snohomish, Snuqualmi, Nisqually and Skykomish used it for salmon fishing. This type of canoe was rarely used in salt water, although the Nisqually sometimes went out on the Sound in it to fish cod. It was a very fast canoe with a flat bottom and bow and stern alike.[99]

Long ago the Snohomish used the Kwī'dɛł instead of the large canoe. This canoe held ten to twenty people. The stern was like that of the large canoe. The bow was made of the same piece of wood as the body, but the stern was put on separately.[100]

The paddles (x̱opt͜ᶜ) used at bow and stern were alike. They were made of maple wood and painted red. The same paddle was used with the various types of canoes. The Snohomish had a lighter, smaller paddle (x̱optᶜładai'ɛlwa's) for women, but the Nisqually had only one kind for both men and women. The type of paddle used by the Sound people differs from that of the Coast Indians.

The Snohomish erected posts with cross pieces on which the canoes rested. The canoe was tied on with ropes. The canoes were always stored in this way, never permitted to stay on the ground. The Snohomish and Snuqualmi used sails of matting. These were used long before the coming of the white people. A bailer of cedar bark was always kept in the canoe. The man in the rear of the canoe did the steering and, among the Nisqually, had a wider paddle.

In addition to the canoes a few household utensils[101] were made of wood. The Nisqually made cedar buckets, the four sides of which were cut in one piece, bent and fastened at the seam with cedar pegs. They never sewed wood with cedar withes as the Kwakiutl did. These buckets were waterproofed with pitch. Some had lids of wood and all had handles of cedar. Boxes of all sizes were made in the same way but none were either carved or painted.[102] The Nisqually and Sno-

[96] According to Waterman, this type of canoe is used for hauling household, possessions etc., in quiet waters and called "freight canoe." Waterman, (a) 15, 17.

[97] Waterman calls this a travelling canoe. His description agrees essentially with the one given above. *Ibid*, 18.

[98] This type was used far inland by the "fresh water" Indians. *Ibid*, 20.

[99] In addition to these types of canoes, Waterman lists a "one-man canoe" (di'twil in Duwamish dialect) and a children's canoe (qe'lbid—same dialect). The former is a smaller model of the light canoe built for one person and used in hunting and fishing. The latter is a double-ended type used for the commonest purposes and given to the children to "practice" in. *Ibid*, 21.

[100] Waterman has an interesting description of the distribution of types of canoes on the North Pacific Coast. *Ibid*, 29.

[101] All of these articles were made by the Chinook and Clatsop. Swan, (a) 163. For a brief summary of the Columbia Valley types, see Lewis, 161.

[102] A very accurate and detailed description of the making of wooden boxes among the Kwakiutl is found in Boas, (a) 60. The process is probably essentially the same. Boxes were made and used by the Klallam for holding water and for household goods. Eells, (a) 628.

homish had oblong dishes (L!ai'ulc)[103] of cedar, maple, or alder.[104]   They were two and one half to five feet long and about three inches deep.   The Nisqually also had spoons of horn or wood with slightly carved handles.[105]

The Sound Indians did not make totem poles.   The inside posts of houses were sometimes carved in a crude manner and more often painted.   The Nisqually used a stone knife with both sides of the blade sharpened.   The narrower end of the blade was tied to a wooden handle with a buckskin thong.   The Snohomish used an unhafted stone knife, sharp on one edge, for food preparation. The Snohomish used a drill with a wooden shaft and a bone point.[106]   This was twisted between the palms.

---

[103] L!ai', wood; ulc, dish. For description of making, see Boas, (a) 57.
[104] Wooden dishes used by Klallam. Eells, (a) 628.
[105] The way the Kwakiutl make horn spoons is described in Boas, (a) 102. Ladles of horn or maple use by the Klallam. Eells, (a) 629.
[106] Stone points among the Thompson. Teit, (b) 183.

DRESS AND PERSONAL CARE

It is difficult to obtain satisfactory information about the original mode of dress of this area because native costume has been in disuse for such a long period. Even from the fragmentary notes at hand it is apparent that there were differences between the shore and inland peoples and between the upper and lower classes in the same group. The Snohomish, for instance, did not have the variety of skins for clothing which were available among tribes that hunted extensively. The buck skin which they used was usually obtained from the Snuqualmi.

DRESS

The poor man of this area wore a blanket[107] in cold weather and went around nude or with only a breech clout in the summer. The well-to-do generally wore buck skin clothing. The Nisqually wore a breech clout of buck skin all year. In the summer this was their only garment. It was fastened to a buck skin belt. Their winter costume consisted of a buck skin shirt (pō'tɛd) which hung to the hips. It had long sleeves with a fringe of buck skin along the underarm seam. Formerly the men wore buck skin leggings that reached from the breech clout to the ankles. The two leggings were never sewed together like trousers. Each was fastened separately to a belt by means of a buck skin strap on the outside of the leg. At the bottom the leggings had a strap that was tied around the ankle. In more recent times the men wore buck skin trousers (yilā'btsid).

Both men and women used shirts and capes of skin, generally with the hair worn on the outside except in very cold when they were reversed. The Nisqually made shirts with sleeves, of groundhog caught in the mountains. The Snuqualmi, Snohomish, Skykomish and Nisqually had bear skin and seal skin capes without sleeves. The Nisqually tied bear skin capes around the necks with buck skin thong and fastened them at the waist with another thong. The alternative way of fastening a cape was with a blanket pin (Xō"ĸ!wadicɛd) of yew wood, deer bone or the legbone of coon. The Nisqually never used beaver skins for garments, but sewed them together for blankets, always with the hair on.

The Snohomish, Snuqualmi and Skykomish wore long trousers which were tied around the knee and fastened into the mocassin with a strap.[108] They were held up by a buck skin belt which passed through holes in the waist band of the trousers. This belt was sometimes made of otter skin with the hair on and lined with buck skin. There were two kinds of shirts, one with sleeves to the elbow, and the other without sleeves. The sleeves were often trimmed with otter skin. The Snohomish men, unlike the women, did not wear a breech clout of cedar bark.

The women of the poorer classes wore a shredded cedar bark skirt (nɛlwa'q) from the waist to just below the knee.[109] They had no covering for the upper

---

[107] Lewis and Clark found a small blanket fastened across the chest with a string, the sole garment of the Tillamook, Chinook, Kathlamat and Clatsop. Lewis and Clark IV, 185.

[108] Although it was not stated in Dr. Haeberlin's notes, I think these were also the extended legging type rather than real trousers.

[109] Kane found this among the Klallam and as the summer costume of Chinook women. Kane, 209, 184. This costume is described by Swan as a work dress, used especially when at work in the water. Swan, (a) 155. Lewis and Clark find the cedar bark shirt in use among the Kathlamet, Tillamook, Chinook and Clatsop. Lewis and Clark, IV, 186.

part of the body. High class women wore a shirt (łupa'a') from the shoulders to below the knees. These shirts sometimes had long sleeves but usually the sleeves were short. The shirts with long sleeves had strings of shell sewn on the under-arm and often had shells or otter fur around the neck. With this shirt went a pair of leggings (bēt'ā's) from the knees to the ankles, where they were tucked into the mocassins. At the knees they were tied around the leg with straps. In rainy weather the women wore a twined cedar bark cape (tcibē'ts!a) over their buck skin shirts. It reached to the hips and was tied together down the front with buck skin thong.[110]

The Nisqually and Snohomish women wore a shredded cedar bark breech clout under a cedar bark skirt in winter; in summer they wore only the skirt, which reached to the knees. Formerly the women wore leggings from the knee to the ankle and with these, the tanned buck skin shirts.

The Snohomish, Snuqualmi and Skykomish women wore both the cedar bark skirts and the buck skin costume.

The Snuqualmi, Snohomish and Skykomish made no basketry hats themselves but bought them for shell money from the surrounding tribes. There were two types of hats, the small brimless, coneshaped hat (nala'qᵘn) twined on a stiff foundation, which they obtained from the Klikitat; and the large hat with a brim (cɛce'ᴱqᵘ) which they bought from the Cowichans.[111] The men among the Nisqually went bareheaded. The women after marriage wore soft brimless basketry hats which they themselves made. They fit the head snugly and did not have the buck skin chin straps which the Snohomish wore on their hats.

In winter both men and women among the Nisqually wore caps of beaver, elk or deer. These hides were either dressed on both sides or if the hair was left on, it was worn on the outside. Little girls wore caps of beaver and boys, caps of coon skin. Both boys and girls sometimes wore strips of beaver wound four times around the head. The Snohomish men wore coon skin caps, the Snuqualmi, caps of wolf, otter, beaver and bear, all with the fur on the outside, and fastened with buck skin straps under the chin. The women never wore these caps. Later they also had bonnets woven of mountain-goat wool.[112] The Skykomish had caps of a young mountain-goat head with the horns and ears of the animal intact. Some of the coon skin caps of the Snohomish also had the ears on them. When the Snuqualmi went hunting they wore a cap of a bear's head.

The moccasins (sᴋ!ā'acid) of the Snohomish[113] and Snuqualmi were made of one piece with a seam up the toe.[114] A separate piece, often decorated with

---

[110] A mat was worn by the Chinook, Tillamook, Clatsop and Kathlamet. Lewis and Clark, IV, 186.

[111] Gibbs speaks of a large conical hat with a brim, the rim fitting the head. This hat was waterproof and painted with figures. Gibbs, (a) 219. This is the northern type of hat used by the Nootka, etc.

[112] One exhibited at the Washington State Museum from Skokomish.

[113] Annie Sam, another Snohomish informant, said that her people did not wear moccasins.

[114] This corresponds to pattern No. 11 of Wissler, which has the following distribution: Naskapi, Montagnais, Ojibway, Cree, Mackenzie, Thompson, Assinboine, Dakota (Teton). Wissler, (a) 144-151. To this distribution the Shuswap should be added. Wissler, (b)

beads, was sewn over the instep. A flap was sewn around the top of the mocca-sin.[115] The moccasins were made of tanned buck skin. Those of the men and women were alike among the Nisqually. They were made either of deer or elk skin, tanned on both sides. Moccasins were never made of beaver or marmot. All moccasins were tied with a strap around the ankle. In winter the Nisqually filled their moccasins with loose deer hair for extra warmth.

PERSONAL CARE

The women of the Snohomish and Snuqualmi parted the hair in the middle from the forehead back to the nape of the neck. The hair hung loose on both sides, covering the ears, and from there on it was braided into one braid on each side. The ends of the braids were wrapped with buck skin and tied. Young girls wore their hair in the same way, only they braided it more tightly to make it grow better. Very little girls had their hair hanging loose. Before marriage a girl's hair was combed and dressed by her mother or grandmother. If she did it herself, her hair would fall out. Deer tallow was rubbed on the hair to make it smooth. At home the men and boys parted the hair in the middle, made a knot on the neck and tied buck skin around it. When the men went to war they braided their hair in one braid and tied it with buck skin to the top of the head. The end of the braid over the forehead formed a tuft which stood erect. It was tied up with buck skin and decorated with shell money. The hair was tied up in this way in war so that the enemy could not get it. Rich men often braided otter skin into their hair for ceremonial occasions. Duck down was put in the hair and it was painted red. When the men's hair grew too long it was cut off at the waistline.

The men among the Nisqually parted their hair in the middle and either braided it or let it hang loose. Sometimes they wore a band of mink or weasel around the head. The men also used hawk and eagle feather in their braids. Each feather was tied separately to a string of sinew. This was no mark of distinction and could be used by any man. The Klikitat used this type of decoration even more than the Nisqually. Often when at work the men tied their hair together at the back of the head to get it out of the way. Shamans and slaves wore their hair just the same as other men did. The women never cut their hair. They braided it in two or three braids and tied the ends with their own hair, never with buck skin. The Nisqually and Klikitat women braided narrow strips of beaver into their hair. These strips were tanned on one side and were about two fingers wide.

Tattooing (SL!e'L!tc) was practised only by the women.[116] The Nisqually

---

105. Hatt finds this type very common among the Northern Athapascans and lists speci-mens from Yellow Knives, Dogrib, Slavey, Chipewyan, Tahltan, Kutchin; also from the Ute, and Skokomish of Puget Sound. Hatt, 165.

[115] For comparison, the informant showed a Yakima moccasin which had a separate sole. The Klikitat moccasins were like the Yakima.

[116] This is also true among the Chinook. Kane, 182. Almost all women among the Lillooet had their wrists and arms tattooed. Teit, (a) 222.

girls were tattooed at the age of ten or twelve years.[117]   The designs used were purely decorative[118] and had no connection with the person's guardian spirit.   The tattooing was usually done on the lower arm or the leg just below the knee.[119] At either end of the tattooed area, waist, elbow, knee, or ankle, a zigzag line was drawn around the limb.   The tattooing was done with a gooseberry thorn and charcoal.   A woman never did this for herself.[120]

Paints were used both as an ornament and to protect the skin.   Both men and women among the Snohomish painted the whole face red to prevent chapping.[121] Sometimes the face was painted with designs relating to individual guardian spirits.   The paint was gotten from the mountain tribes by trade.   The Snuqualmi also secured red paint (xalā″ltsid) from east of the mountains.   It was ground on a flat stone and mixed with a little water.   Then deer grease was added to make it adhere to the skin.   Yellow paint (qwā′dzālōs) was obtained from the stream beds.   It was dried but not ground.   Instead of mixing the paint with deer grease, the grease was rubbed on the face as a base and the paint was applied afterwards.   In hot weather these paints were used to keep the face cool.

Young Snuqualmi girls before marriage painted the face as follows: a streak of red paint in the hair just over the forehead: red paint over the eyebrows, and on each cheek, a semi-circular line just over the cheek bone.   After marriage the whole face was painted red from the eyebrows down.   The forehead was left untouched.

The Nisqually, especially the women, painted their faces just for decoration. The paint was made from a clay found in pools.   The clay was burnt over a fire to make it more red and then ground to a fine powder and mixed with grease. Paints were used all year round and were not associated with special occasions.[122]

The Snohomish women did not use labrets or nose ornaments.   The Nisqually used no labrets but the high class women wore shell money in the septum.[123] Neither the men nor the women wore abalone shell in the nose.   The nose was usually pierced when a child was about five years old.   The Snuqualmi women also wore long pieces of shell money in the septum.[124]   More general was the piercing of the ears for ornaments.   The Snuqualmi had holes all around the helix.[125]   New holes were pierced when the old ones were worn through.   Rich men often had an ornament in each hole.   Children had their ears pierced at the age of eight.[126]   The hole was made with a bone awl (Sʟ!qau′d).   The piercing

---

[117] Evidently at maturity.   This is also the time chosen by the Lᴋuñgᴇn women for tattooing. BAAS 1890, 574.

[118] Karok women tattooed three narrow fern leaves on chin.   Powers, 20.   The Skagit used lines on arms and face. Bancroft I, 211.

[119] Arms, legs and cheeks were tattooed by the Chinook. Bancroft, I, 229. Arms, waist and chin were tattooed by the Lᴋuñgᴇn. BAAS 1890, 574.

[120] The entire statement about tattooing agrees with the information in Swan. Swan, (a) 112.

[121] The women around Puget Sound painted with vermillion clay. Bancroft, I, 210.

[122] The Chinook painted only on special occasions, as at the death of a relative or at starting out on a war party. Kane, 184.

[123] Shell money was worn as nose ornaments by the Chinook, Kathlamet, Clatsop and Tillamook. Lewis and Clark, IV, 187.

[124] The women around Puget Sound wore nose ornaments. Bancroft, I, 211.

[125] BAAS 1890, 636 Shuswap.

[126] BAAS 1890, 574 Lᴋuñgᴇn.

was done by an old person who received a present of shell money for his services. Sinew was kept in the hole to prevent it from closing up, but no medicine was applied. Ear piercing often took place in connection with receiving the second name. Only the women among the Nisqually wore ear ornaments. Abalone shell was suspended from the ear by means of a strip of buck skin.[127] Sometimes two shells were suspended from separate holes in the same ear. Shell money also served as ear ornaments.[128] In recent times the Nisqually have been wearing necklaces and bracelets of shell. This was not done long ago. The high class Snohomish, Skykomish and Snuqualmi wore shell necklaces with deer hoofs attached for special occasions.

While bathing, the body is rubbed with rotted twigs.[129] The Snohomish used yew leaves and the Snuqualmi used fir for this. A bunch of shredded cedar bark was used as a towel. A white stone found on river banks was used as soap.[130] The Snohomish had combs (cpa'ts) of yew wood. The teeth of the comb were about three inches long, the whole comb measuring about eight inches. For pulling out hair on the face, tweezers made of deer horn were used. The end of a horn was split in two pieces which were riveted together by a peg of horn.[131]

SWEAT LODGES

The sweat lodge[132] used by the Snohomish was about seven feet long, six feet wide and four feet high. Usually it was occupied by only one person.[133] There were some a little larger accommodating two, but more than two never went into a sweat lodge at the same time. The lodge was made of a framework of sticks which were covered with twigs and brush. This was covered with dirt.[134] The lodge was not built over a pit;[135] there was only a slight depression in the floor for the hot stones. The door opening was covered with blankets and mats. The fire was built outside the door.[136] Here the stones were heaten and then rolled into the sweat lodge. The hot stones were sprinkled with water by hand, the water never being squirted from the mouth.

The sweat lodge was always built beside a creek or river so that the bather could plunge immediately into the cold water.[137] The Snohomish never went into salt water after a sweat bath. The sweat lodge was considered the personal prop-

---

[127] Another informant stated that abalone shell was not worn in the ears.

[128] The Lillooet used shell traded in from the Coast tribes as ear ornaments. Teit, (a) 220.

[129] An instance of this occurs in the "Salmon Myth."

[130] Thompson used a "white soapy clay obtained from the shores of certain lakes." Teit, (b) 228.

[131] The Thompson have tweezers of one piece of horn bent over, or two pieces tied together at one end. Teit, (b) 227.

[132] See "Origin of Sweatlodge," JAFL 37, 414.

[133] Eells, (a) 624 Twana. Quinault, four together in lodge. Farrand, 104.

[134] Thompson, Handbook, 661.

[135] Differs in this respect from northwestern California and Nez Percé. Kroeber, (a) 86. Spinden, 198.

[136] Nez Percé, Spinden, 198.

[137] Karok, Powers, 12.

erty of the man who built it. If another wished to use it he had to ask permission. The sweat lodges of shamans were just like those of others.[138]

Shelton, a Snohomish, never heard of a woman using a sweat lodge. Among the Nisqually, however, women and little girls used them. The Chehalis had sweat lodges like those of the Nisqually.

The sweat bath (wux^{u}tan) was used for medicinal rather than ceremonial purposes. Sometimes herbs were taken while sweat bathing. Often, when the bather plunged directly in the cold creek, he would vomit. This was considered good, for it cleansed him thoroughly. After sexual intercourse a man was considered impure, (su'l) tired and weak. A sweat bath cured him from this and purified him.

---

[138] The only sweat lodges of the Twana were used by the shamans. Eells, (a) 623.

LIFE OF THE INDIVIDUAL

Although the Puget Sound people were not as given to ceremonial as their northern neighbors yet each of the crises of an individual's life was marked by some departure from the normal routine.

BIRTH CUSTOMS

When a Snuqualmi woman was about to give birth to a child she went out to a little lodge built away from the communal houses.[139] This lodge, covered with mats like the summer house, was about eight feet square and six feet high. After the birth of the child it was torn down.

The Snohomish woman was also rigidly secluded at the birth of each child. If a birth was imminent while the people were camping in the summer, the pregnant woman withdrew from camp just as she would from the communal house. The Snohomish birth lodge was like the summer house except that the latter had the fire outside. Before leaving the lodge the woman burned the mats on which she had been lying. The framework of the house and the covering mats were folded up and stored for further use and regarded as the property of the individual family. The woman stayed in her lodge twelve days. During this period her husband stayed there with her,[140] but slept on a separate bed. He brought her water and tended the fire.

The three Nisqually informants contradicted each other as to the place where the pregnant woman stayed. Henry Martin and Henry Sicade agreed that she stayed in the communal house with a screen of matting put around her. Mrs. Kate Mounts, however, said that the woman retired to a lodge shortly before confinement and stayed there for fifteen days, although now women stay only five days. This lodge was covered with mats, and, when out camping, with brush. The woman sat on moss and ferns which were afterwards tied up and put in a tree. The menstrual lodge was not used for this purpose.[141] To give birth in such a lodge would be a "terrible thing."

The Nisqually were always active during pregnancy, as this was supposed to lead to an easy birth. A few families used medicine to stunt the growth of the child and make delivery easy.

The Snuqualmi woman was attended by her mother, or if the latter were dead, by some intimate friend. Occasionally a midwife was called in, but she did not have the powers of a shaman and could not perform like one. She was paid for her services. The husband was not allowed in the lodge during delivery but could come in soon after.[142] Several old women attended the Snohomish woman at delivery. Among the Nisqually, midwives were present.[143] They were

---

[139] This was also done by the Tsimshian, Boas (d) 530; Tahltan, Emmons, 100; Blackfoot, Wissler, 28.
Kodiak women stayed in lodge for ten days. Jackson, 111.
[140] Northern Maidu, Dixon, 229.
[141] Hupa women, Goddard, 51; Northern Shoshoni, Lowie, 214; and Northern Maidu women, Dixon, 229, all use the menstrual lodges.
[142] Husbands were excluded among the Tahltan, Emmons, 102; Northern Shoshoni, Lowie, 214; Blackfoot, Wissler, 28; Kwakiutl, Boas, (c) 652.
[143] Midwife officiated among the Tahltan, Emmons, 100; Kwakiutl, Boas (c) 650; only a chief's wife had a midwife's services among the Chinook, Boas, (e) 242.

paid except by poor women. A shaman might come and leave a prescription for the woman but he never stayed during delivery.[144] The midwife administered whatever he ordered. The midwife had no powers similar to those of a shaman.

The Snuqualmi woman was often given medicine to hasten delivery. Cashmere knew these medicines but would not tell them because they were worth "lots of money." He had bought the knowledge from another.

The Nisqually deemed it most important to keep the patient warm. This was done by having her sit on mats with hot ashes or stones underneath.[145] Warmth was necessary lest the "blood get thick" and cause death. If a woman had an exceptionally long period of labor a shaman might be called in to knead her abdomen, but this was seldom done. Various teas were given to women in labor. Some were: Johnny Jump-ups (viola semper verens), of which the whole plant was boiled and steeped in water; sprouts of the small wild rose, nettle buds, or willow and June plum bark were boiled together.

The Snuqualmi woman wrapped the baby in soft shredded cedar bark The infants of wealthy people were wrapped in mountain goat skins beside the bark. The baby was bathed every day in an oval dish of maple wood in which the water had been heated by means of hot stones.

The Nisqually also washed infants in lukewarm water. They wrapped them in fur, never in cedar bark. The Nisqually gave the infant no food for two days, but only lukewarm water.

The cradle board was the same for boys and girls. It was a flat cedar board with strips of buck skin attached through holes burnt in it. A piece of cedar board was strapped over the forehead to flatten the head.[146] Underneath this board was an oblong padding of shredded cedar bark wrapped in buck skin. This was held down by buck skin straps. Rolls of cedar bark were put under the neck, the arm pits and under the knees when the child was strapped on the board. The child stayed on the cradle board for one and a half years. The Nisqually also used a hammock of rope and bear skin, which was fastened to the house posts. The child was rocked by means of a rope attached to the mother's foot. The Nisqually women used the cradle board especially while working and traveling, when they had it strapped to the back. The Snuqualmi hung the cradle to a forked stick about six feet long. The stick was planted firmly in the ground and the cradle suspended from the forked end. When the baby cried someone rocked it. In earliest infancy the baby's nose and ears were pulled to make the child beautiful.[147]

As soon as a Snohomish woman was strong enough after childbirth she bathed every day. The Nisqually woman did the same, taking care not to wet her breasts. She always tied something over them. The women of the Nisqually, Snohomish and Snuqualmi steamed the breasts before nursing the child. Hot rocks were laid on the ground and sprinkled with water. The woman crouched

[144] The Tahltan shaman also did not serve at births. Emmons, 100.
[145] Hupa, Goddard, 51.
[146] Cowlitz and Chinook, Kane, 180.
[147] Kwakitul. Boas, (c) 669. Hupa. Goddard, 52.

over them and let the steam rise to her breasts. To confine the steam more thoroughly she held a blanket over herself.

During her seclusion in the lodge, the Snohomish woman was attended by her husband. He lived there with her and was not permitted to go near other people. While living there with his wife he had to bathe morning and evening and keep exceptionally clean. On the other hand a Nisqually, especially if he was a fisherman or hunter was not allowed to go near his wife during her confinement. Only old women were allowed to visit her lodge.

There were several food taboos for the pregnant woman and her husband.[148] For twenty-five days after the birth of the child, the Snohomish parents were not allowed to eat fresh fish or meat. The woman among the Nisqually was not allowed to eat fresh fish or meat, but her husband was permitted to eat these things provided he stayed away from his wife. Among the Snuqualmi, on the other hand, both husband and wife observed no food taboos during the woman's pregnancy.

While a Nisqually woman was secluded in her lodge and afterwards, she used a head scratcher for four to six weeks. If a boy was born the mother's hair was washed by some woman on the fourth and eighth day after the birth. When a girl was born the hair was washed on the fifth and tenth day.

The Nisqually looked upon twins with great disfavor. When twins were born the people began to wail and went to the house of the parents and took away their food, clothing and other property. Some property was given in return after some time. The things which were taken away were divided among the people who took them.

Abortion was often practiced by unmarried women. It was never done by applying pressure, but by drinking medicine to force premature birth. This potion was the secret of certain women who only administered it for good pay.

PUBERTY CEREMONIES

The chief difference in the several accounts given below is in the length of time the girl is secluded. There may have been tribal differences, but the fact must also be taken into account that since the coming of the whites the period has been curtailed considerably.

Among the Snohomish an adolescent girl was isolated in a lodge[149] a short distance from the house. After fasting for ten days she was sent out to bathe, two nights in succession. The thirteenth day she was given a drink of rotten fir wood mixed with water. After this she could eat. In this account no mention is made of looking for a guardian spirit.

Another informant stated that during the first menstrual period the girl stayed in the mat lodge for twenty-five days in absolute seclusion. On the

---

[148] The Tsimashian woman after delivery abstained from fat food. Boas, (d) 530. The Hupa woman abstained after delivery from fresh fish and meat, forty days for a boy, fifty days for a girl, and sixty days for a miscarriage. Goddard, 51. The Northern Shoshoni woman abstained for several days before the expected birth from meat and fish. Lowie, 214. The Northern Maidu man and woman eat no meat or fish for 5 days after delivery. The woman continued her taboo until she left the lodge. Dixon, 229.

[149] Tsimshian, Boas, (d) 450; Tahltan, Emmons, 104; Kadiak, Jackson, 111.

twenty-sixth day a woman who possessed a spirit, that would make the girl eat, for she was all dried up inside, came to feed the girl with a clam shell. During her seclusion the girl sat on old mats which were buried, never burned, after use. She had to keep her teeth and nails very clean, and used a head scratcher.[150] If the village had a stockade around it the mat shelter was erected outside and away from the trail. The girl was not allowed to have a fire. When she returned from her seclusion her parents called their people together for a feast and presents. Blankets were torn up and the pieces distributed. At this time only the parents' tribe was invited. Other tribes received word of a girl's maturity through hearsay.[151]

NAMES

A person usually had a series of names during his lifetime. At birth a child was given a nickname[152] by which he was known until he was about ten to twelve years old. Then he received the name of one of his ancestors.[153] Later if he distinguished himself in any way he received a surname proclaiming his prowess.[154] A man might also get a name from his guardian spirit.

Each tribe had its own set of names and within the tribe, each family considered the use of certain names its own privilege. It was an offense for a person to take the name of an ancestor of another family. If this occurred, the offender had to give a potlatch for the family whose name he had taken. The same is true in regard to taking a name from another tribe. In this instance the potlatch was given for the family from whom the name had been taken, not to the entire tribe. A girl could not take the name of her father's brother's wife unless the woman consented to have her name used while she was still alive. If she were dead her people might object because the woman was not an ancestor of the girl who wanted her name. Two cousins never took the name of a common ancestor. Quarrels often arose over this and were usually settled by payment from one person to the other.

If the name of a deceased person is mentioned the offender had to pay the relatives of the deceased. A dead person was referred to as a relative of some living person. A man never spoke of his own dead father or son for at least a year or two after the death occurred. The nickname of a dead child was also avoided for a while. If later, another family wanted to use the same nickname they could do so, provided they were careful not to let the bereaved family hear it.

---

[150] Tahltan, Emmons, 104.

[151] The feast was given by "opposite" family among Tahltan. Emmons, 105; Kadiak, Jackson, 112.

[152] A Haida child is given a name he is ashamed of to make him accumulate property and change his name. Swanton, 284.

A Kwakiutl child is named after the place of his birth. Boas, (c) 653.

A Tahltan child is named after a maternal relative. Emmons, 103.

[153] Between the ages of 8 and 15, a Tahltan child receives a name from the family of the maternal uncle. Emmons, 103.

The Northern Shoshoni name a child at 12-14 years. Lowie, 211.

The Twana and Klallam take a name from a direct paternal ancestor. Eells, (a) 656.

[154] A Blackfoot youth gets a name after his first war party and after worthier deeds may change it for a more dignified one. Wissler, 17.

When a baby received its nickname, it was not necessary to give a pot-latch. Rich people occasionally did it. But when a boy or girl took the name of an ancestor, it was expected that a potlatch be given. Even people of low rank would not keep their nicknames after they reached maturity. If they could not afford a feast they took the name of a parent or grandparent, in which case it was not necessary to pay for the name with a potlatch. If a boy took the name of his grandfather who was still alive, the old man gave the potlatch. The same was true in the case of a father. If the child took the name of his grandfather who was dead, the father gave the potlatch. An orphan paid for the potlatch himself, if he was rich enough. These naming potlatches could be given at any time of the year.

There were some principles governing the choice of names. Cashmere said that had he become a shaman he would have taken the name of his father, Little Sam, who was a powerful shaman. In this Cashmere would not have paid for the name with a potlatch because he would have earned it through acquiring shaman's spirits. Had Cashmere become a warrior, he would have taken the name of his grandfather, who had been a famous warrior.

Among the Nisqually at a naming feast, a man did not announce his own name. He hired somebody to do it for him.[155] The Nisqually did not invite other tribes to naming potlatches as did the Cowlitz and Chehalis. The latter had a man from another tribe call out the new name.

At marriage a woman never took the name of one of her husband's ances-tors, although she might get a new name from her own people. Children of parents from two tribes could be named from either tribe. The inheritance of a name had no connection with the inheritance of a guardian spirit or property.

Some concrete examples of names follow:

Snuqualmi Jim had dzā"wēnus as a baby name. No potlatch was given when he received it. He did not know where his father got the name for him. At the age of twenty-five his maternal grandmother gave him the name of her father, saying that Snuqualmi Jim looked like him. The name was Kwayaī'itc which was a "big" name. No potlatch was given when he received this name because he was a policeman.

Little Sam had as a nickname, Kwī'aha. He did not like to have it used. To address a person by his nickname after he had acquired a real name was considered an offense. The name which Little Sam got from his ancestors was s'ā'datsut.

The names of one man of the Nisqually were the following: smū'täs, nick-name; chief Stī'lequem, after marrying a chief's daughter from another Sound tribe; s.o'swē, a surname referring to his prowess; i'nɛmła, Thunder, a name he got from his guardian spirit.

Some Nisqually nicknames are:

lo'gùᵇ, son of Mrs. Mounts' half uncle.

'e"exud, nickname of many boys.

---

[155] Among the Blackfoot the Chief Weather Dancer announced a change of name at the Sun Dance. Wissler, 17.

tsē'e''eχud, girl's nickname.

ō''olax, name, especially for an orphan.

ts!χwā'los, "she has small eyes," nickname for a girl, but a boy might
    be called the same.

tᴇkwā'di', "deaf," boy's or girl's nickname.

ts!aχᵘ, "little," girl's nickname.

łā'daila', "girlie."

Names of adults (inherited):

xēduwa, Mrs. Mounts' eldest daughter, inherited from Mrs. Mounts'
    grandmother.

wanä'nät, Mrs. Mounts' eldest son, inherited from Mrs. Mounts' great
    grandfather, a Cowlitz.

k!wanasā'pab, Mrs. Mounts' second son, meaning "man who has house
    with carved posts" (Cowlitz name).

kwē'cäł, Mrs. Mounts' second daughter; means "it's fog;" guardian
    spirit name of Mrs. Mounts' mother's aunt.

waha'n, Mrs. Mounts' third son, a Cowlitz name.

ᴌē'ᴌ!kwadōt, Mrs. Mounts' mother (Cowlitz).

bā'tstakub, grandfather of Henry Sicade.

punō'iχᵘ, Nisqually man's name.

k!wanēbat, Nisqually name, brother of ᴌe'cχaix.

waχwilō't, Nisqually man's name.

ts!ō'tstēlēts!a', Nisqually woman's name.

so'tqaxad, Nisqually woman's name.

qai'q!ᴇblot, Nisqually woman's name.

nᴇt!ā'k!ᵘ, Nisqually man's name.

INSTRUCTION OF CHILDREN

The old people gave the children advice, telling the boys what to do to be
good men and teaching the girls how to be clean, make good baskets, be good
wives, and how to be hospitable. Such instruction was called go'sa'lad. Among
the Snohomish a man took his boys of six years or more out to the water every
morning and made them bath and rub themselves. This makes them strong
men. This practice did not apply to girls. Mothers made cedar bark dolls for
girls, while the men made model canoes for little boys.

The Snuqualmi told their children to hold out their arms in a storm so that
the wind could blow into their armpits to make them odorless.

When a Snohomish child lost his first deciduous tooth he was told to run
to the woods with it and call for dog salmon teeth while throwing his tooth in
the river. With the second he was to call for beaver teeth; with the third for
deer teeth. Frank Leclair, who did this when he was a child, said that he had
good strong teeth on account of obeying this custom. William Shelton said
that adults do not believe this, but tell it to the children to keep them from
worrying about their lost teeth.

When Little Sam, a Snohomish, was a boy, he was a great favorite of Annie

Sam's (his future wife) grandfather, an old Snuqualmi. The old man taught Little Sam how to make a pheasant trap. For this Little Sam's mother gave the old man two blankets.

Among the Nisqually a girl's seclusion lasted from six to eight months.[156] During the first five to nine days the girl fasted. Then she could eat vegetables and dried meat and fish, but nothing fresh.[157] During her stay in the mat shelter a rich girl had a woman slave with her. Girls whose parents could not afford this were visited by an old woman, older than their mothers.[158] During the entire period a girl's face was painted red. Her head and face were covered in such a way that she could look only straight forward. When a girl first went out to the shed, her hair was braided in two braids which were rolled up closely to the head and tied. Each month the braids were let down a little lower. Several strings of buck skin were tied around one wrist and one ankle. Each month one string was untied. The girl also kept count by making a knot in a buckskin strap attached to one of her baskets. While in the lodge the girl was kept busy making mats and baskets, all her work being given to an old person. The dress she wore was also given to an old woman. During this period the girl went out at night looking for a spirit. After this period of seclusion was over the lodge was moved to another place and used regularly as a menstrual lodge. During the first menstrual period the lodge was always occupied alone.[159]

MENSTRUAL CUSTOMS

After the first period a Snohomish woman went to the menstrual lodge only for the duration of the period. During this time she could drink water and eat dried meat. An old woman brought her food. If a woman should keep her menstruation secret, a shaman curing in the house where she was would become aware of it because his spirit would not work.[160] A hunter would not hunt nor a gambler play while his wife was in the menstrual lodge. If the wife or daughter of a warrior was in the menstrual lodge, he would not start out with a war party for his spirit was weak at that time and he might easily be killed.

The Nisqually women went to the menstrual lodge for five days. During this period they bathed every day and rubbed themselves with twigs. They had to bathe in a pond or a spring, never in a river where the people fished. Several women often stayed in one lodge together. The lodge was moved to another place at each period, but the same framework was always used. The Nisqually women did not have to restrict their diet but they had to be careful not to pollute the food of others, never giving anything they cooked to another

[156] The Tahltan secluded a girl from six months to one year. Emmons, 104. A Kadiak girl was secluded for one year. Jackson, 111.

[157] Tahltan, Emmons, 104.

[158] The Tahltan girl was attended by her mother, aunt or another old woman. Emmons, 104. Kadiak, Jackson, 111.

[159] Compare these customs with those of the Klallam (Gunther, 232), which resemble much more closely those of the northern Salish, Nootka and Kwakiutl.

[160] Among the Blackfoot medicines would not "work" if a menstruating woman came to the place. Wissler, 29.

person. Everybody avoided the menstrual lodge, especially hunters, for the animals could smell the uncleanliness and would not allow themselves to be caught. Hunters even made detours around the menstrual lodge so as not to cross the trail the women used. Should he by accident infringe on these regulations he had to bathe and scrub and even go to a shaman to purify himself.

While women were in the menstrual lodge they continued their work. What they made could be used by everybody, but the things a girl made during her first period were given to old people. Slave girls and women as well had to resort to the lodge during their periods.

MARRIAGE

Marriage among these Puget Sound tribes, as is so frequently the case, was a contract between two families. Theoretically there was a difference between the marriage regulations of the upper and lower classes, in that the upper classes practically insisted on tribal exogamy, while the common people with no social connections had to be content to marry within their own group. Before the coming of the whites, the Nisqually never married within their own tribe, and not even into another village of the tribe. This regulation theoretically applied to everyone, but was only rigidly enforced in the upper classes where infringement was fined. The fine was paid to the girl's relatives, and after such amends they would frequently consent to let their son-in-law live with them.

Among the high class people there was strict watch over young girls. A chief's daughter until marriage was usually accompanied by a slave, either a man or a woman. Yet on the other hand, a high class girl was not always ostracized for having a child before marriage. When an unmarried girl became pregnant she had to tell who was the father of her child. If the liaison was with a low class man and the girl insisted on staying with him, her father might be ashamed and send her and the man away to live.[161] If an unmarried girl became pregnant and her parents were willing to take the man as their son-in-law, he stayed with the family. If they objected to him he would have to pay the girls' parents. Should he fail to pay this fine he might be killed by the girl's relatives.

Marriage was always accompanied by the exchange of presents and visiting back and forth. The parents of the groom generally took the initiative among the Snuqualmi. A man, accompanied by the son whose suit he was pressing, would visit the parents of the girl and present gifts. If these gifts were acceptable, the marriage was consummated at once, the groom staying with the bride at her home. After about one week the bride's people took the newly married couple to the groom's family and brought food and presents with them. The groom's family responded with gifts for the service of having brought the young couple back.

Among the Snohomish the groom's people also made the first presentation of gifts, an act which was called s'ɬaleqᵘ and was not regarded as a potlatch. Later the girl's parents gave presents in return (s'e′tsamaɬ). These two acts bound the

---

161 A common incident in the folktales of this area. JAFL 37, 414.

couple together. Both sides at these occasions distributed blankets and other property among their own relatives and friends. If the family was of sufficient social standing to make the marriage an occasion, the chiefs and leading men present made speeches, telling the young people how to act in their life together. After these exchanges of gifts the parents of the young couple would loan each other property (cacxᵘe'l) without potlatch obligations.

Such procedure was only possible among wealthy people. Common people who could not afford gifts married on mutual agreement with no ceremony. Often a man promised gifts, but the actual giving might not take place for several years. In contrast to the northwestern Californian tribes, an interchange of gifts was not compulsory.[162]

The following are some accounts of actual marriages known to the informants and illustrate very well the customs involved.

The chief of the Suquamish at Port Madison wanted to marry his daughter to the son of the Puyallup chieftain to strengthen the union between the two tribes and avoid war. After negotiations, the Puyallup chief came to Port Madison and gave a potlatch, bringing provisions that could not be secured in the Suquamish country. Each family provided for a family of guests. Several months later the Suquamish went to Puyallup for a similar ceremony. Such a return should never be hurried. When the Suquamish came to Puyallup they camped on one side of an imaginary line and the hosts gathered on the other. After the bridegroom's father, the Puyallup chief, had sent gifts to the bride's people, the girl was brought to her husband's side and gifts sent in return. Among these gifts was a very fine canoe with its many paddles each carried by a girl. It was agreed that this canoe should be used for visits from one tribe to the other and that as many people of the Puyallup as there were paddles in the canoe should go to live with the Suquamish. After the chiefs finished exchanging gifts, the two tribes as a whole exchanged presents. When all the property had been distributed the young couple stood up and clasped hands (koda'kgwil). The chiefs made speeches saying that the union was complete. The day was finished with a feast and contests in diving, swimming, spear throwing, while through the night there was gambling and dancing. The next day the gathering disbanded.

When Henry Martin, a Nisqually, married, his bride's father had come and asked that he marry his daughter. Since some of her relatives objected, her father urged an immediate marriage. Martin gave his father-in-law five horses and fifty dollars in money,[163] for which he received nothing in return until a year later, when his father-in-law gave him three horses. Martin's father and brother also each gave a horse to the bride's father. At the time of the marriage Martin's parents-in-law gave presents to their own relatives but none to his people, while Martin's family kept only two horses for themselves and gave all their others to their own relatives. There was the usual feast at the wedding.

Little Sam, a Snohomish, gave his bride's mother forty blankets, two slaves and a canoe as marriage payment for Annie, a Snuqualmi.

---

[162] Among the Karok, Yurok and Hupa a payment is necessary to legalize the marriage. Powers, 22, 56, 75.

[163] The Karok paid eighty to one hundred dollars for a bride. Powers, 22.

In another instance a Nisqually man wishing to marry a Cowlitz woman sent one of his friends to her people to ask their consent. When this had been granted he went with his friends, taking many horses with them. After distributing presents and feasting, the Nisqually went home, taking the Cowlitz bride with them.

On another occasion Henry Martin and his cousin went to Skokomish to get a man's consent for a marriage between his daughter and a Nisqually man. They took with them a gift of fifty dollars. When consent had been given, the Nisqually bridegroom and his people went to Skokomish for the wedding and the feast. They returned to Nisqually with the bride.

These few accounts show clearly several important points in Puget Sound marriages. Tribal exogamy is of prime importance to the upper classes. The giving of gifts is rather an exchange than a payment for the bride. Wherever it is mentioned, the permanent residence is patrilocal even though there may be a short stay at the bride's home.

After marriage, blankets and mats were the common property of husband and wife; otherwise whatever a woman made was her own. She had the privilege of selling or exchanging her wares and keeping the returns for herself. In the same way hunting and fishing gear remained the man's property to deal with as he saw fit.

After the death of her husband, a Nisqually woman generally married his brother or cousin, while a widower married his wife's sister. If a woman did not marry one of her husband's relatives, she usually returned home with her children, and after several years married into another family. A widower also allowed several years to elapse before remarriage. It was not necessary for the survivor of a couple to return to the family of the deceased any of the property received at marriage.

When a Snohomish couple separated, an attempt was always made to reunite them. If a woman was abandoned for laziness, her people had to return part or all of the gifts received at the time of her marriage. Both parties of a divorced couple could remarry, but the one known to be at fault could rarely marry again in the same tribe.

When a woman was mistreated, the chiefs could decide if a divorce was justified. If they decided to the contrary they would urge the couple to stay together.

If a Snuqualmi woman left her husband without his consent her people had to return the marriage gifts, but if he agreed to the separation such restitution was not necessary.

The following account of domestic relations is interesting. Leschi had three wives, the eldest of which had relations with a young unmarried man. Leschi became angry and cut off part of his wife's hair, whereupon she ran away to Leschi's brother. Leschi followed, intending to kill her, but his brother protected the woman. Finally the couple became reconciled, and to "smooth matters over" Leschi gave his father-in-law three horses and received in return one slave.

At a second marriage there was no elaborate ceremony and no exchange of valuable gifts.

BURIAL AND MOURNING CUSTOMS

In this area there are many forms of burial, both aerial and in the ground, but there is no cremation. The usual form of burial used by the Snohomish and Snuqualmi was placing the wrapped body in a canoe.[164] The body was dressed in clothing, wrapped in skins, blankets and cedar mats and tied with swamp grass.[165] Strings of shell money were put on a wealthy person and small bits of personal property were wrapped with the body, but no food. The bottom of the canoe was covered with cedar shakes and the body, lying on its back with the head toward the west, was set in. It was covered with cedar shakes. Holes were bored in the bottom of the canoe to let the rain drain. The canoe was either put up on cross pieces that were laid on four posts to which it was roped, or it was tied into a tree with hazel withes. Sometimes it was set under the trees in the forest and a shed built covering the body. Women as well as men were buried in canoes.

When the canoe was not used, the body was wrapped in the same way and laid on a scaffold about three feet above the ground.[166] A shed with one pitch or gable roof was built over the scaffold. There was no carving or painting on the grave shed itself, but frequently the ceremonial stick which had been used in spirit dancing by the deceased was set beside the grave.[167] Bodies were sometimes laid on a platform built in a tree. This was especially done for slaves for whom canoe burial was too costly. A very poor slave's body was thrown in a hole and covered with earth.[168] The Snohomish and Snuqualmi never put bodies on the ground with a box over them.

The body of a chief was sometimes kept in the house for several days with shaman watching over it. The body of a poor person or a slave was kept just outside the house and covered until burial.[169] The Snohomish, Swinomish, Skagit and Snuqualmi never carried a corpse out by the door, but instead made a hole in the wall near where the body was lying and carried it out through that.

The Nisqually practiced inhumation, using a grave from two to nine feet deep.[170] Sometimes cedar bark was laid in the bottom and the body placed directly on that, while in other instances a coffin was made of cedar shakes. The body was covered with cedar bark and the grave filled. Rocks were placed on the grave to keep animals from destroying the corpse.[171] Occasionally the Nisqually used canoe burials and set the canoe in a tree. Often the body was simply wrap-

---

[164] Canoe burial was found by Swan at Shoalwater Bay. Swan, (a) 70. Chinook, Swan, (a) 185. Twana, Eells in Yarrow, 172.

[165] Yarrow, 177.

[166] Makah, Yarrow, 178.

[167] Chinook and Chehalis, Yarrow, 179.

[168] Yarrow, 178; Bancroft, I, 221.

[169] Thompson, Teit, (b) 327.

[170] The latter depth seems excessive, especially since these graves were supposedly dug with digging sticks.

[171] Another informant stated that no rocks were put on the grave; only two sticks were set in the ground, one at the head and one at the feet. The Thompson place rocks on the grave but give as their reason the fact that it marks the site. Teit, (b) 329. Yarrow, 178.

ped in cedar bark and put in a tree without further covering.[172]   When such a burial decayed and the bones fell out, they were often reburied in a grave.

For all forms of burial, the Nisqually dressed the body in the person's best clothes and wrapped it in blankets of deer and elk skins. A shaman was the most competent person to wash and dress the corpse, but if no shaman was available some member of the family did it. He also put the body in its final resting place. Bits of personal property and shell money were placed with the body, but some of the possessions of a wealthy man were given to relatives and to the poor. Such things were always given to old people. Other property, not disposed of in this way, was buried outside of the owner's house. The corpse was never kept in the house longer than a day and a night, and sometimes it was buried immediately after death. A person with a special spirit was hired to carry the corpse out of the house. It was taken out through the door. As with the northern tribes, the Nisqually placed no food on the grave.

A widow or widower went to bathe every evening, never in the day time, for several weeks and rubbed his body with twigs. Parents did the same at the death of children. This however was not done when a brother or sister died. At the death of parents, husband, wife, child, brother or sister, both men[173] and women cut their hair[174] twice. Half was cut, four or five days after the death occurred, and four or five days later the remainder was cut to mourning length, just below the ears.[175] The hair was cut by an old person and the cuttings were buried secretly or hidden. A head scratcher was worn on a string around the neck. A person who had been in contact with the dead had to bathe and change his clothing. He was not allowed to touch food for several days, but was fed by others.[176] This did not apply to the people who were just present at the burial. After the loss of her husband or child a woman bathed more often to wash off the touch of the dead person. Women often fasted in mourning.

Children were told to keep away from the corpse lest the ghost get them.[177] Adults did not believe this but said it only to frighten the children. Graves were not avoided by adults but young people rarely visited them. The old people went out to the graves to wail. For a certain number of days after death occurred a morsel of every kind of food eaten was thrown into the fire for the deceased. If a person who had recently died was referred to the people began to wail.[178]

[172] Kwakiutl, Boas, (c) 1120.

[173] Two other informants stated only women cut their hair.

[174] Twana, Eells in Yarrow, 173. Karok widow cuts hair close to the head, Powers, 33. Lillooet cut hair across the back, Teit, (a) 221. Tsimshian, Boas, (b) 534.

[175] This is an ambiguous statement of which I have found no further explanation. Whether one side of the head is cut first and then the other or whether the hair is cut twice in the length could not be determined. Thompson, Teit, (b) 333. Near relatives of the dead cut their hair among the Haida, but if a chief dies the whole village does it. Swanton, 52.

[176] The impure eat with sticks. Thompson, Teit, (b) 331.

[177] Twana and Klallam, Eells in Yarrow, 176.

[178] Mentioning the name of a deceased person had to be atoned for with the payment of blood money. Karok, Powers, 33. Tolowa and Klikitat do not mention name of deceased person. Power, 68; Gibbs, (a) 405.

After the loss of a close relative people wailed for months. Men did not wail as much as women.[179]

When an important chief died two or more slaves were hanged or strangled to death[180] and put in the canoe with him. For such a sacrifice, the slaves were never shot or cut to death. The bodies of the slaves were wrapped in mats and one was placed in the bow, the other in the stern, while the chief's body was laid in the middle of the canoe.[181]

The property which remained after the appropriate things had been buried with the corpse, the Nisqually gave to friends and relatives,[182] especially to those who came to wail. There were no women hired especially for wailing, but each of those who came received a gift. The person who gave away the property of the deceased would expect to receive something in return on the death of a similar relative of those who received these gifts, but he would not expect more than he gave. This distribution of property took place while the body was still in the house.[183] A feast was given to the friends and relatives who had come to mourn.

After a body had been buried a while, it was taken out and put into another grave, the decayed flesh being put in one box and the bones in another.[184] At this time another potlatch was given. Since this involved great expense, only the wealthy could afford it. If the bones fell out of the bundle placed in a tree, a man with a certain spirit power would pick them up, wrap them in blankets of mountain-goat wool and hang the bundle back in the tree. Only a person with this spirit could do this; an ordinary person would die if he attempted it. He was paid for his services. If a person could not give his dead relative a proper burial on account of his poverty, he would, when he became wealthier, take the body from its resting place and bury it in a proper manner. He would hire a man with power to do this. At this time a potlatch was given and the man who performed the burial would receive the largest share. A burial was considered proper if a large amount of property was buried with the body. When the Nisqually moved away, they often dug up the bones of their dead and took them to their new home to bury them there.

---

[179] Twana and Klallam, Yarrow, 176. Women paid for wailing. Tsimshian, Boas, (b) 534.

[180] Gibbs cited in Yarrow, 180.

[181] The Thompson killed slaves at the grave or buried them alive in the bottom of the grave. Teit, (b) 328. Chinook, Yarrow, 179.

[182] Thompson, Teit, (b) 331.

[183] Another informant stated that the feast and distribution of property took place after the body was buried.

[184] Swan gives an instance of reburial which occurred near Shoalwater Bay when he was there. Swan, (a) 73. Thompson, Teit, (b) 330.

SOCIAL LIFE

SOCIAL GROUPING

Among the Snohomish there were two distinct social classes, the free and the slaves, the latter generally being war captives and therefore belonging to another tribe. Within the free group, two classes were distinguished, but there was no essential difference between them. The high class (sīyam'atsiłtamix^u), to which the chiefs and their children belonged, had greater wealth and more important names than the middle class (p!aL!aL!atsiłtamax^u). The slaves (stō'naq^u) did not figure socially.

The children of the high class people belonged to the class of their parents, but sometimes a chief would marry a middle class or slave woman. Then there would be constant trouble in determining the exact standing of the children. Such children were called qEqē'l', "tied to something low," referring to the origin of their mother. This stigma would cling to them regardless of the high rank of their father.

KINSHIP TERMS

There is only slight dialectic difference between the kinship terms listed here for the Snohomish and those of the other groups discussed in this paper. This list was secured from William Shelton by the present writer about six years after Dr. Haeberlin did his original work at Tulalip. Shelton is apt to over-formulate, but there is nothing here which does not check with other systems obtained from coast Salish groups.

hēwilēa'ok	any person beyond the great great grandfather
qwēya'obc	great great grandfather
tca'biak	great grandparent
tsapa	paternal or maternal grandfather
skou tsapa	specifically maternal grandfather
kiya	paternal or maternal grandmother
bad	father
sk!ou¹	mother
kassi'^{k}	father's or mother's brother while parent is living
yala'b	father's or mother's brother after parent is dead or father's sister after parent is dead
pus	father's sister while parent is living
alstc	mother's sister
ska	older brother
so'qwa	younger brother
sitlepspu's	parallel or cross cousin, general term
sitlepspu's teteqwa'l	parallel or cross cousins whose mothers are sisters
sitlepskassi'	parallel cross cousins whose fathers are brothers
bEda'	a grown son

bɛbɛda	a small son
kake'	a baby boy
ts !ekake'	a baby girl
stalał	sister's or brother's son or daughter; stobc, man, or słanī, woman, may be added to explain term

Upper class people always use the diminutive in speaking of their children to show that they are not boasting about them. In giving a speech, a man may refer to his son as bɛbɛda' although he is grown, thus classing him with low people, but his listeners will know that he is proud of him. In this way he is identifying his son with the poor people instead of looking down on them.

In speaking of close relatives, kinship terms are used in preference to names.

SLAVERY

Captives taken in war were enslaved. If a man of high rank was captured, his people might send a good orator of a neutral tribe to his captors and intervene, offering ransom. Such a payment might be two or three ordinary slaves.[185]

The children of slaves remained in the slave class.[186] They were nevertheless sent out for a guardian spirit just as other children. If a slave boy found a powerful spirit and became successful in fishing, hunting,[187] or gambling, his owner claimed his game and his winnings. In return, the slave was well treated. He did not have to sleep on the ground by the fire but was allotted a bed near his master.[188] When a slave obtained a warrior's spirit, he went to war with his master and cared for him when wounded.

If a slave among the Snohomish died while in captivity, he would not go to the land of the dead of the Snohomish because he did not know the trail. He went to the land of the dead belonging to his own people and once there, he returned to his former status of being a free man. However, a slave born among the Snohomish would go to the land of the dead and remain a slave there.

Little Sam said he never heard of a slave stealing. A lazy slave was whipped unmercifully but never killed as punishment.[189] As a rule, chiefs did not treat women slaves as concubines. There were, of course, exceptions to this, but they were disapproved. A child of a slave woman and a man of high rank was regarded as half a slave and looked down upon.

It was claimed that none of the Sound tribes killed a slave to bury under the house post when a new house was built.[190]

Among the Snuqualmi slaves were considered only good enough for getting water and catching salmon. They were not allowed to hunt.[191]

[185] Tahltan, Emmons.
[186] Gibbs, (b) 188.
[187] Kwakiutl, Boas, (c) 840.
[188] Tsimshian, Boas, (d) 435.
[189] A man killed his wife's slave for lying to him. Tsimshian, Boas, (d) 435.
[190] Tlingit bury slaves under house posts. Hunt, 282.
Tsimshian bury slaves under totem pole. Boas, (d) 435.
[191] Kwakiutl sent slaves seal hunting. Boas, (c) 840.

The Nisqually sometimes killed a slave at the death of a chief.[192] Among them a slave was addressed either by his own name if he made it known or by the name of the tribe from which he was captured.

GOVERNMENT

The Snohomish had one head chief for their tribe, although there were two villages, one at Priest Point and the other at Hebolb. The chief lived at Hebolb, for the other village was composed only of low class people. At one time Lɛ'tsxk!ē'dɛb was the head chief. He was the only Snohomish who had a tiō'łbax̣ spirit. His father had been head chief before him and his eldest son succeeded him. This was the prescribed order, but if an eldest son was worthless the younger brother would take his place.[193] t!ē'xtɛd, the son of Lɛtsxk!ē'dɛb, who became chief, was the paternal grandfather of Little Sam. The father of Little Sam should by rights have succeeded to the chieftaincy, but he became a shaman, which made him ineligible. His cousin, who was a warrior, therefore became chief. Although a shaman could never become a chief, he could give his opinions in meeting.

The Snohomish had besides the head chief, four or five sub chiefs who were generally brothers or cousins of the chief. Should a chief's son be too young to assume office at the death of his father, his paternal uncle would rule for him until he was of age. Later, when the young man became chief the uncle would continue to act as his adviser. When a chief was dying, he named his successor. If the people approved, the man became chief. A woman could never be chief.

A head chief was visited by other tribes, who came in canoes and brought gifts. The chief was expected to return the presents with interest. If a hunter secured a large quantity of game or fish he gave the chief some, expecting a return some time. But he was not forced to share his game with the chief and he would give him no more than he would give any old man he respected. It seems that a chief had but little hunting and fishing to do for himself.

A tribal meeting might be called any time of the year by the head chief. The meeting was always held at Hebolb, and the people of Priest Point came over. Slaves were sent out as runners to announce the gathering. At such a meeting the head chief addressed the people. Any man of importance could give his opinion. Slaves were allowed to be present, but they could not speak. Questions of intertribal relations were discussed at these gatherings. If a warrior wanted to go to war, he asked the approval of the head chief. If the latter disapproved, he would state his reasons and convince the other warriors not to join. Should the warrior insist upon going and should he gain the support of his friends, the head chief could not force him to stay at home. The majority ruled in every case, and even the head chief had to submit. It is said that the Samish once killed their head chief because he always tried to force his will on the others.

---

[192] Kadiak, Jackson, 112.
[193] Gibbs, (b) 184.

Among the Nisqually, the chieftaincy was not hereditary, but the chief was elected by a general vote, sometimes for only a few years, often for life. If the election was nearly a tie the women, boys and girls (after puberty) were called in to vote. Generally only the men took part in tribal meetings, which were presided over by the chief or a shaman, the necessary qualifications being age and dignity. The leader opened the meeting with a speech giving the purpose of the gathering. At such meetings the members of the council which advised the chief were elected. To vote, each man rose and gave the name of the candidate he favored. The council was composed of seven to thirteen men, always an odd number so that there would not be a tie. A decision of the chief could be recalled by the general vote of the people.[194]

The council members did not live in one village but were scattered throughout the tribe. They met with the chief at some central meeting place.

Each village had a prominent man as leader, but he was not necessarily a member of the council.

A Nisqually chieftain had no claim to the game and fish secured by his people. He was exceedingly democratic, living and working just like any of his people. Hunters often gave him of their game, but this was no obligation.

When two tribes had a dispute about the murder of a member of one tribe committed by that of the other, the two sides came together and camped some distance away from each other. Each tribe had one or two spokesmen who were very good orators and especially paid for their services. The people of each tribe discussed the case and told their spokesman what to say. Then the spokesman addressed the other tribe. If payment was demanded for the murder, the two spokesmen bargain about the price. If the dispute was not settled, war followed. Should, however, the two tribes come to an agreement, then gifts were exchanged and each tribe tore up blankets and gave pieces to the people of highest rank in the other tribe. The Snohomish, Skagit and Skykomish had the custom of tearing blankets. The Snuqualmi never did it. The pieces were unraveled and the wool woven into new blankets.

GROUP GATHERINGS

The Potlatch. One of the most important social functions was the potlatch. The system was not as highly formalized as it was farther north among the Nootka and Kwakiutl, yet its etiquette was rigid and its social obligations well understood. The potlatch was a great feast given primarily for the distribution of gifts to the guests. Each person receiving gifts at such an occasion was under obligation to his host to invite him to his next potlatch and to give him an adequate gift in return. The potlatch has been under ban so long that it is difficult to obtain any of the finer details of its operation any longer.

[194] This entire account of government, especially that of the Nisqually, seems to me oversystematized. Ed.

The occasions for potlatches among the Snohomish and Snuqualmi were the following:

1. When receiving a new name.
1. In summer when the salmon began to run. (sgwē′gwē′)
3. At death.
4. When the corpse was reburied. (spa′q!eksɛm)
5. After a successful hunt.

Potlatches were generally given in potlatch houses, built especially for the purpose. The sgwē′gwē′ potlatch was given only in a potlatch house which had been built by a man having the tiō′łbax̣ᵘ or heyida spirit. Such a house was never inhabited. At the death of the owner it was abandoned unless his son also had one of these two spirits. No other man of the tribe, even if he had these spirits, could take possession of the house. The potlatch house was larger than the ordinary dwelling and was always built on the river bank or directly on the Sound. It did not have to face in a definite direction.

The Snohomish had a sg̱wē′gwē′ potlatch house at Hēbō′lb (Blackman's mill) owned by lɛtsxqē′dɛb. Si'a'ł (Chief Seattle) owned one of these houses at Port Madison and there was also one at Lummi. They were all owned by men who had tiō′łbax̣ᵘ. Si'a'ł had hired men to build his house.

Potlatches could be given by the rich men, who vied with each other in giving away large amounts of property and in making even larger returns. If a man received one blanket, at his own potlatch he returned two or three. Such generosity made a man famous. At a potlatch the guests also distribute property among their own friends.

Among the Nisqually when a young man or young woman took the name of a dead ancestor, friends were called in for a feast and some old guests received presents. This feast lasted several days.

The sgwē′gwe′ or cultus potlatch was held in the old times by the following tribes: Chehalis, Cowlitz, Skykomish, Klallam, Snohomish. It is definitely stated that it was not held by the Nisqually or Puyallup until recently. There also seems to be some difference of opinion as to whether the Snuqualmi or Skykomish had it. Today it is still held (on a much smaller scale) by the Klallam, Snohomish, Lummi, Swinomish, Twana, Skagit and Suquamish.

The sgwē′gwē′ was held in summer when the salmon began to run. It could only be given by a man having the tiō′łbax̣ᵘ or the heyida spirit and was given in a potlatch house. Neighboring tribes were invited to the feast. They brought gifts of fish, deer, blankets or shell money, to the man giving the potlatch, but he always tried to give more than he had received. At this affair everyone tried to show the "power" he had. One man swallowed hot bullets and made them come out at his side.

At a sgwē′gwē′ potlatch each tribe present performed its war dance (sqwā′-tsɛb). This was danced on roof boards which were laid over three or four canoes that had been tied together and were afloat near the shore. While a tribe danced, the members gave presents to the spectators. Later they received more in return from other tribes performing.

At the potlatch orators held long speeches. As an orator talked the people piled up gifts before him. Everybody was anxious to give something to a famous speaker.

Sometimes a person had a lucky spirit which brought him much wealth but he could not by himself give a cultus potlatch; so he would pay a man with tiõ'łbaxᵃ or heyida to give the potlatch for him. Often it took a man several years to save up enough property to give such a big potlatch.

At the death of an individual all his property that was not buried with him was given away. Anyone who received these gifts was expected to give back at least the same amount when a similar relative of his died.

The potlatch held at the removal of the corpse was limited to high class people, for it was a costly affair. At this time the body was taken from one grave, wrapped again and put into another grave. A man with a special spirit was hired to do this.

Small potlatches (słā'dap) were held at any time when a hunter had been especially successful. He invited his friends for a feast and gave them presents. There were no sklaletut performances at these potlatches, just plenty of food.[195]

Spirit Singing: Any time from the middle of November to the beginning of January a man's guardian spirit came back to him and urged him to sing his spirit songs and perform his dance. Many sklaletut travelled around the world all year and returned at this time, but the spirits which did not travel also came to their owners. When the spirit came the man felt sick, but this was not regarded as an ordinary illness and a shaman was never summoned. As soon as this illness came, the man could hear his spirit song ringing in his ears. Then he would call his friends together and they helped him sing and dance. If his friends did not know his spirit songs they followed him as he sang them and learned. These dances varied greatly in length, for a man sang as long as his spirit commanded him to do so, often several days. At this dance no shaman was present.

When the singing was over, if the man were rich, he would give many blankets to his friends who had helped him. If he were poor, his friends would help him just the same, but they would not expect any gifts. Although these dances were all held in the same season (spegpugud) they were arranged so that the people could go around from one to the other.

There is very little doubt that this spirit singing takes the place of the winter ceremonial current among the northern Indians. In each place it centers around the concept which is most important to the group: in the north, the secret society; in Puget Sound, the guardian spirit.

There seems to be some difference of opinion as to whether these people had any social dances. Cashmere stated that the Sound Indians had no social dances, but that the Klikitat had them. Another informant claimed that among the Nisqually social dances were very important. They were never given alone, but usually in connection with a shamanistic performance. Both men and women participated, but they did not dance together.

---

[195] Further details on the Klallam form of potlatch may be found in Gunther, 306.

DIVERSIONS

Games: Whenever a group gathered, whether it be at a potlatch or just a chance meeting, it was usually an occasion for games, especially gambling games. Even today when large numbers assemble at berry picking or in the hop fields in the summer, there are regular evenings given over to the old games, especially slahal. At potlatches the women watched the men's gambling games and helped in the singing, but never participated. They, however, had games of their own in which they staked such articles as they also used for potlatch gifts. In addition to the gambling games there were athletic contests and children's games.

słaha'łb was a man's game.[196] The opponents A and B sit about fourteen feet apart, each at the end of his mat, which is unrolled about one-third of its length. This mat is called tsila'lyan. It is pinned to the ground by sticks (tsō'x !ᵘlatci) about twelve inches long, of pencil thickness, and carved at one end. Six sticks go with each gambling mat. Experienced gamblers are very particular to see that the ground is smooth under the mat.

Wooden discs about the size of a silver dollar are used. There are ten, nine of which are white and one black, or the reverse. The disc which is different is called stō'mic. A and B kneel at the end of their mats facing each other. The rolls of the two mats touch in the middle. Each man has his supporters clustered about him. The two sides agree on the one to start. The player (A) takes the discs, wraps them in shredded cedar bark, shakes them and tears the bark apart so as to have 5 discs in each bundle. These two bundles of cedar bark he puts on the mat before him and commences to move them around quickly with a circular motion, each hand moving counterclockwise. The other player, (B) must guess which bundle does not contain the stō'mic. He guesses by pointing his finger at the bundle. The player, A, then unwraps the ball at which B pointed and rolls the contents down the mat toward B. He unwraps the other ball and placed the discs in front of himself. If B guessed correctly he receives the discs and plays; otherwise A continues.

In one corner of a mat near the roll are the tally sticks ('sxa'ts!) on a small board (sxɛła's). Each stick is four inches long, round on one side and flat on the other. They are made of a hard wood, usually ironwood. Before starting the game, the number of sticks, which must be an even one, is decided upon. Two of these sticks are dark, and these are laid in the middle with an equal number of light sticks to each side. They are called kᵘłʟ, meaning half way. One of the players must win all the sticks. Except for marking the halfway place, the dark ones have no further significance.

The counting is as follows: If B guesses wrong the first time A receives two sticks. After that he receives only one stick for each wrong guess. If B guesses right the first time he receives no sticks, only the right to play. Then if A guesses wrong the first time B plays, B gets two sticks, provided he himself had guessed wrong two or more times while A was playing. If he guessed wrong only once, he receives only one stick now.

---

[196] Compare with Klallam. Gunther, 275.

Slahal[197] is essentially a man's game, though it is sometimes played by women, using smaller cylinders. Slahal is played with four cylinders of bone, of a size that two will fit comfortably in a closed hand. Two of these cylinders are white (sto'bobc, men) AA'; and two have bands of black (słaładei, women) BB'. The players guess for the white ones. Two leaders play against each other and with them sit their followers, who beat time with sticks (tc!a′x^{u}adid) on a plank (L!pai′′atsid) before them. The two parties sit facing each other, a few feet apart. The leader of the first side L^1 guesses in which hand L^2 has A, and vice versa. Each leader guesses by slapping his breast with his left hand and pointing with the forefinger of the right hand. If both guess wrong they continue, each with one set of cylinders, hold one cylinder in each hand. If L^1 guesses right he gets the two cylinders, and one tally stick. Now one side has four cylinders. The leader shakes them and gives one pair to each of two people on his side. These men shake them and take one in each hand and move their hands at full arms' length from and toward the body. The leader of the other side guesses. If he thinks the cylinders are distributed BAAB, that is BA in the right and left hands of one man and AB in the right and left hands of the other, then he slaps his breast with his left hand and makes a downward motion with the forefinger of his right hand. If he guesses ABBA he hits his breast and stretches out the thumb and forefinger of his right hand horizontally. If he guesses ABAB, he motions to the left with his right hand always with the left one on his breast. If he guesses BABA, he motions in a similar way to the right.

If the leader guesses correctly his side gets the four cylinders. If he guesses only one hand right he gets two cylinders.

The number of tally sticks (sxa′ts!) is agreed on in advance, Perceval stating that as many as eighty are played for. Skookum George said only ten to twenty were used. A side must win all at least once, often four or five times if the stakes are high. The tally sticks are slender pieces of wood pointed at one end and stuck in the ground before the plank on which the men beat time. When all four cylinders are on one side and the leader guesses only one hand correctly, then the side which has the cylinders gets one tally stick but forfeits two cylinders. If the guesser misses both, the other side gets two sticks. The side that has the cylinders in play sings and beats time, the other concentrates on guessing.

st!at!aba[198] is another guessing game, but one played only for amusement, not for gambling. Both adults and children play it. One side had a little ball of mountain-goat wool about half an inch in diameter. It was passed from person to person until finally someone hid it in his hair or his clothing. While the ball was being hidden the other side covered their faces with their blankets. Then they began guessing. Each person who guessed wrong moved to the end of the line. If they failed to guess, the same people hid the ball again. If they guessed correctly they hid the ball.

---

[197] Probably the same as game called "La-Hull" by Swan in his description of the Chinook. Swan, (a) 158. Klallam, Gunther, 274.
[198] Klallam, Gunther, 278.

smẽ'tali[199] is a woman's[200] game widely known in the Puget Sound region. There are four beaver teeth, two with black lines (stōbōbc, men) and two with black dots (słałada, women).[201] The under side of the dice was plain. Beans or sticks were used as counter.[202] One woman had to get the forty tally sticks four times to win, but not necessarily in succession. One of the słałada had a strip of cloth or skin tied around it. This was called k!ēs.[203] The throws were:

1. Highest—k!ēs up, other three down or k!ēs down, other three up, equal four sticks.

2. All up or all down, equal two sticks.

3. Both stōbōbc up or both slalada up or vice versa, equal one stick.

4. All other throws equal nothing.[204]

A woman played until she threw number four; then she passed the dice on. Some women "knew how to throw."[205]

tcᴇtcwi'lts,[206] shinny, was played in the summertime on the beach or the prairie. It was always an interibal contest with slaves, canoes, shells, or blankets as stakes. Each tribe selected twelve to twenty of its best men and a captain. The men were naked except for a breechclout. Each man had two sticks[207] curved at one end.[208] With the stick in his left hand he defended himself. The ball was of cedar or fir wood,[209] a little larger than a baseball. The object of the game was to drive the ball across the adversary's goal at the end of a field from six hundred to eight hundred yards along.[210] The ball was started in the center. Pushing a player aside or tripping him on one's stick was permissible. To win, one side had to put the ball over the goal line twice in succession. stēoq lu"[211] was a game like shinny, but played without sticks. The ball was large and soft, made of buck skin, about one and one-half feet in diameter. It had two loops of buck skin at the sides. There were fifteen to twenty men on a side. The object was to carry the ball over the adversary's goal line. A field was marked off on the beach. The person who had the ball ran with it in his arms. The ball was started in the center of the field by being thrown up by one

[199] Chinook, Swan, (a) 158.
Bella Coola, Klallam, Twana, Puyallup, Snohomish, Chehalis, Quinault, Cowlitz, Lummi, Skagit, Squaxon, Sooks, Nisqually, Shuswap, Songish, Thompson. Culin, 155-157.
[200] Klallam, Gunther, 276.
Designated as a woman's game among the Nisqually, Snohomish, Thompson, Twana, Culin, 155-157.
[201] Klallam, Culin, 155.
Songish, Culin, 157.
[202] Snohomish, Culin, 156.
[203] Bella Coola, Culin, 155.
Nisqually, Culin, 156.
Songish, Culin, 157.
[204] Twana, Culin, 157
[205] Twana, Culin, 157.
[206] For distribution, see Culin, 36; description of Klallam game, Gunther, 278.
[207] Makah, Culin, 616.
[208] Culin, 616.
[209] Culin, 617.
[210] Field lengths: Miwok, 200 yards; Mono, 1400 yards and return; Makah, 200 yards. Culin, 617.
[211] Klallam, Gunther, 278.

of the leaders. The men on one side threw the ball to each other. Tripping an opponent was permitted. The ball must go over the line twice in succession to win.

sada'k was a dancing game in which a person in a squatting position danced between two lines of spectators. The person who endured longest won. Boys and girls, also women, played this together.

stĕtxō'twa'l was a tug of war which the boys and girls played against each other. They used a pole to pull on, not a rope. Children did this for fun, but often young men played it for stakes.[212]

sasxwa'ᵇ was a contest in broad jumping, learned from the Klikitat. It was played by the young men for stakes. There were several on each side. The first man jumped from a stick on the ground as far as he could and marked his landing place with another stick. The second man must jump farther. If he jumped on the stick he lost.

When foot races were intertribal, gambling was connected with them. The runners were paid and the spectators did the betting. Races were usually held on the beach or the prairie. A race was run either in one direction or around a pole and return. Foot racing originated, it is claimed, with the race of the mountain-goats for the daughter of qeqe.[213]

Wrestling also was an intertribal competition. Wrestlers were hired and the spectators bet on the winner.

Children, as among all peoples, amused themselves by imitating their elders. They played at curing patients like shamans and used for this, at least among the Nisqually, basketry rattles filled with pebbles. These were never used by real shaman. Boys shot with small bows (ts!ā'tsuts) and arrows (t!ē'ttsuᵇ), which they made for themselves. They shot for distance, winning arrows from one another. Boys also had foot races. Young boys and girls played together, but as they grew up they were kept apart.

In addition to these pastimes they had various games which they generally played by themselves, but in which adults occasionally shared. The hoop and pole game (sbɛbe"), an adult game in so many Indian groups, is here played only by children. In playing the children would "just for fun" sing the heyida spirit songs. This, incidentally, shows that the children knew the songs before going out for a guardian spirit.

syē'yi[214], derived from yē'yi, to laugh, was known as the laughing game and played by boys and girls. There are an equal number on each side. One person on one side holds a small crooked stick. The two lines stand facing each other a little distance apart. The person with the stick calls over to a person in the opposite line: "Come get this stick!" The person must then come over to get the stick without laughing. The line having the stick sings:

"yēgēlɛsxai'ab"
"Shame on you, you are laughing."

[212] Klallam, Gunther, 278.
[213] JAFL 37, 384.
[214] Klallam, Gunther, 277.

If the person laughs he must go back to his line; if he gets the stick without laughing, he takes it over to his side and they sing the song. In order to win, it is necessary for all people on one side to have gotten the stick four times.

SMOKING

One Nisqually informant stated that his people dried the leaves of the kinni-kinnick[215] and smoked them. They made some pipes with stems of alder or maple. The stems were about four to six inches long. Often they bought pipes from the Klikitat. Women smoked sometimes, but not often.

Another informant claimed that the Sound Indians did not smoke until after the coming of the whites, when they obtained black stone pipes from the Klikitat. The scabby boy was the one to introduce smoking.[216]

[215] Northern Shoshone, Lowie, 213.
[216] JAFL 37, 433.

RELIGIOUS LIFE

SPIRITS

Most important in the religious life of the Puget Sound Salish were the personal spirits. There were two distinct kinds of spirits, the sklaletut and the xᵘdá'b. The former is the spirit of the layman and either brings luck in the acquisition of wealth and, through it, rank, or else it is a warrior spirit that makes his war enterprises successful. The xᵘdá'b spirits are the shamanistic spirits which help the medicine man effect cures. Henry Martin, a Nisqually, spoke of a person with a sklaletut spirit as "just harmless," distinguishing him from a shaman who might be dangerous. The informant did not know how these spirits looked in visions. Only the persons who acquired these various spirits could describe them. And even then the description might vary, for the same spirits are supposed to act differently toward each person they meet.

A feature common to all spirits is that they have songs, each spirit having words and tunes of his own. Most sklaletut spirits travel around the earth in an anticlockwise direction, completing the circuit once every year. On their journey they gamble or trade, and their owner's luck would vary with that of the spirit in his enterprises. The spirits come back in November at spegpegud (winter dance) time. At this season every person who has a spirit becomes sick, due to the spirit's return. Even if his spirit is one of the kind that do not travel he becomes sick at this time. When he began to feel ill, he would sing his song, perform his dance and knock his long sklaletut pole against the ceiling. This was continued for several days, during which period the person fasted and slept very little. At this time a man's friends came to help him sing. At the end of the period the man usually gave a potlatch. As soon as the spirit left him on his next year's journey, the man would recover. A shaman was not called in for this, because the person was not really ill. There was a clear distinction between this and physical illness.

It was impossible to inherit a spirt without doing something personally to acquire it. Among the Snohomish, a boy usually got the spirit that had been in his family before, either in the paternal or maternal line. If a spirit was inherited in this way, the boy nevertheless had to fast and bathe. On the other hand, it was not necessary for an ancestor to have a spirit in order that a boy might acquire one. Among the Nisqually the same general principles held good. If a person had an ancestor who was a great shaman, for instance, he might have a predisposition for getting a shamanistic spirit.

The regular way of getting a spirit was through personal experience, usually at puberty but often also later in life. Women could get spirits as well as men, but they got only the less powerful ones, for they were not strong enough for a big spirit. The powerful spirits only came to men who could fast long and endure many hardships. A man could go out to seek a spirit even after he had had sexual intercourse, but during his quest he had to maintain absolute continence. He also had to purify himself by fasting, bathing and taking sweat baths.

In the realm of spirits there was reflected the social system of their believers. A powerful spirit would appear only to a man of high rank. If a slave should get a powerful spirit he would become a high class person, but this did not happen often, for a person of low rank usually got only a small spirit. Cashmere however tells of a Samish Indian whose father was partly slave and whose mother was of high rank. This boy looked for tiō'íbax̣ᵁ, one of the most powerful spirits. He went through the usual procedure of covering a rock with saliva and then diving into a great whirlpool with it. This boy dove into a pool in the Snuqualmi River and dropped the rock. When he came up tiō'íbax̣ᵁ and other spirits came to the Samish. Tiō'íbax̣ told the boy that he could only give him half his power— "half his house"— because his father was of slave descent. The boy could not do everything that others with this spirit could accomplish. For instance, he could not make game drop dead at his door.

Both boys and girls were sent out at the time of puberty to find a spirit. If the children did not want to go, they were whipped and received no food. In the evenings the old people told the children about the various spirits so that they would recognize them. A child's father and grandfather instructed him especially as to the nature of the experience to expect, but a child would not always come home with the spirit he set out to get. Often when he went out for a sklaletut, he would bring home a shaman's spirit. Likewise a boy may get a warrior spirit even if his forefathers had been shamans and vice versa. Orphans listened to the advice that other children got from their parents.

Children were sent out in the spring, generally March and April, when the spirits were most likely to send out their servants to meet people seeking them. Many of the Sound Indians sent their children out only in stormy weather, for it was believed that at that time the spirits came to the surface and were easier to get. The Snuqualmi, however, sent children out any time during the winter. The children were not sent out in the summer because the parents were afraid that the abundance of berries about them might make them cheat, for fasting was absolutely necessary. The child was given no provisions whatever. He wore a cedar bark belt tightly around his waist so as not to feel his hunger so keenly. The Nisqually sometimes sent children out in summer when it thundered.

Before a child went out to seek a spirit an older person would set a marker at a certain place, telling the child to get it. This would prove that the child had been there. Cowlitz prairie was known as a good place for getting certain spirits. Sometimes a boy heard a spirit crying. This happened very rarely, but it was certain when he did hear it that he would get the spirit. When the child went out he was given a firebrand made of a roll of cedar bark. He made a fire that served as his headquarters and from this place he went out in different directions looking for a spirit.

Little Sam's grandfather was a great warrior and he was anxious that his grandson should acquire a warrior spirit too. He taught Little Sam how to dive for such a spirit but it was of no avail, for the boy returned home with a shaman's spirit. Besides this shamanistic spirit Little Sam had others. The following is a description of how he obtained one of his spirits.

Little Sam was sent out by his grandfather to get a spirit. He was given a firebrand of dry cedar bark and told to stay away as long as it burned. It burned ten days, during which time Little Sam fasted, but he met no spirit. He came home and was given a firebrand that burned fourteen days. Again he fasted and bathed, but no spirit came to him. He returned home and received another firebrand. This one burned fifteen days, and during this period he finally met a spirit. He saw a man going up to the mountains from the prairie and the spirit was coming down from the mountains. The spirit was a white man carrying an arrow in one hand, a slahal bone in the other. His gift to Little Sam was that all white men would like him. When Little Sam was asked at the end of the narrative for the name of the spirit he commenced crying and said if he told it he would die. Afterwards, however, he was prevailed upon to disclose the name. It was sta ā'yewi

To obtain some spirits it is necessary to dive into deep water. Often a boy floated down a river on two logs, carrying a heavy stone with him. When he got well into the water he covered the stone with saliva and dove into the water with it. This made him sink to a great depth. When he awoke he would find himself lying on the beach. Sometimes a boy made a raft and fastened himself to it by a long cedar rope. He would then dive with his stone and leaving it on the bottom, would pull himself up by the rope. When the boys dove in deep water in the Sound there was supposed to be danger from sharks. To protect himself the boy was given a sharp stick of ironwood which he carried stuck in his hair. When a shark attacked him he forced the stick into the shark's mouth. Little Sam told of this and he claimed that only the Snohomish knew of it. This stick was kept in a secret place in the house so that people would not see it. Not even the Priest Point Snohomish had knowledge of this thing. Little Sam's grandfather gave him one when he was sent out to seek a spirit.

Sklaletut Spirits: The following pages list the spirits described by various informants. They are grouped according to the powers they bestow.
Hunting and fishing:

hu'x^uhui'dnan: A general name for all spirits that bring luck in hunting, fishing and gathering clams.

cau'ł: Badger spirit. Little Sam acquired this spirit at the same time that he got the tɛbā'k!wak, shaman spirit. He fasted for ten days until his intestines were all clean. Then he made a badger trap. He found the badger and tɛbā'k!wak in one hole and he slept four days and four nights with the two in his arms. This gave him the power to catch badgers.

sg^ulōβ: Pheasant spirit. Little Sam got this spirit when he learned how to make a pheasant trap. He fasted for several days and then he found a white female pheasant. He slept with this pheasant. Then he slept for two days and nights in the bushes close to the pheasant trap. The grandfather of Annie Sam went out to get Little Sam and carried him home. He let Little Sam sleep in the house for five days. Then the old man told the boy to bathe. He mashed some salmon and made soup in a basket for the boy. Little Sam tried three times to eat the soup but each time he vomited. The fourth time he was able to eat the soup. It was necessary to get this spirit in order to catch pheasants with the trap.[217]

xᵘa'ltqam: This spirit has no house, but lives in a big canoe in the middle of the sea. His servants look out for young men who are seeking spirits. These servants bring the youths, who must be of high rank, to the canoe at night. A man with this spirit has power over all kinds of clams. When he has danced and sung with his friends, the people go out and find piles of clams on the beach, through the power of this spirit.

sx̣wu't: This spirit was a small species of bird. It was powerful for hunting. Little Sam had it.

sgᵘdī'lătc or gudē'latc is a spirit known to the Snuqualmi and Snohomish. It stays under the water all the time, either in a river or in the Sound, and never travels. It is good for catching fish, especially salmon. Women can also have this spirit; in fact the first person to have it was Johnny Wheeler's great grandmother, a Snohomish. She was out in a canoe, fishing with a net attached to a pole. She looked into the water and saw many fish. Then she fainted. When she regained consciousness she found a board. After this, fish became plentiful in the river on which her family lived. This woman gave the spirit to her daughter, who in turn passed it on to Johnny's mother. When his mother died Johnny went out to get the same spirit. He lay on her grave, sleeping and fasting for four days. The board used in the dance is a flat piece of wood about one and one-half feet long, painted red and black. Before the dance board was used it was heated at a fire into which some fat of dried salmon had been thrown. This was called "finding the spirit." The single board is used by the Snuqualmi, but the Snohomish use two boards, one larger than the other, representing an older and a younger brother. Two men dance with each of these boards, each putting one hand through the hole in the board. The two men who dance with the larger board—the older brother—lead the dance, which always progresses in a counterclockwise direction. Should it be danced in the opposite direction, the owner of the spirit would soon die. The owner of the spirit never dances with the boards himself. He sits to one side and sings his songs while four hired men do the dancing. These men each receive one blanket and some other present for their services. Other people also sit around and sing. They likewise receive presents. The singing and dancing lasted four days and four nights. The songs were always sung four times in very fast tempo and four times slowly.[218]

In November near spegpegud time the owner of this spirit spreads out a large portion of his property at a certain place near the shore. Then he invites his friends to go and get the property of his spirit.

This spirit, besides procuring fish, also helps in finding the dead body of a

---

[217] For myth, see JAFL, 37, 413.
[218] Singing a song four times and with increasing rapidity is also done in the ha'mats', a ceremony of the Kwakiutl. Boas, (c) 426.

person lost in the woods or drowned. A searching party of this kind would start out by singing the songs of the spirit.[219]

tc!ā'dzo': next to sgudeletc this spirit is the best for getting fish, especially salmon. It is also good for hunting ducks, seal and sturgeon, but has no influence over deer, elk or clams. It looks like a decoy for ducks. It does not travel, but lives in the water with sgudeletc, to whom it seems to be closely related.

q!wo'xq!: This spirit is known to the Snuqualmi and Snohomish. It helps catch deer and also cures its owner when he is ill and helps in gambling. It lives up in the mountains and travels around the world. It will appear to both men and women. This spirit has a pole and a feather hat. The pole, which is from ten to twelve feet long, is painted and carved and has shredded cedar bark tied around it. When the spirit songs are sung the pole would dance up and down of its own accord and knocks against the roof of the house. This pole was given to a man who had fasted ten days and nights. Either two or four poles were used and these, like the boards of the sgudeletc were divided into elder and younger brothers. Likewise the songs were sung four times in very fast tempo and four times in slow. Johnny Wheeler, a Snuqualmi, had this spirit.

yilbī'x^u: This spirit was almost as powerful as heyida and a young man had to be of high rank to acquire it. yilbī'x^u had servants who looked like men, not animals, and a house in which there were fish and animals of all kinds. These animals did not have to be hunted. yilbī'x^u's power was so great that they dropped dead when they passed his house. A man possessing this spirit sang:

"Call your people in and let them help you up,"

The next day his people would see the animals and the fishes come just as though they were tame. The animals died in the woods and the fish on the shore. This spirit also enabled its owner to tell where a great school of whales could be found.

Industrial spirits:

ts!a'q: This spirit may be acquired by men and women, but women got it more often than men. It helped a woman make good baskets and mats, thus making her rich. A man, it helped in hunting and fishing. ts!a'q travelled around the world, and also had a house and a servant. One informant stated that a person must be of high rank to acquire this spirit, but this was contradicted by another. Women went out in the woods to get this spirit just as men did. To men it appeared from the west, to women, from the east. When the servant saw a person who was looking for a spirit, he said to his master from outside the house, "I have a young man here who seems to be good." Then the youth was brought in the house. The spirit gave various kinds of implements to the persons seeking him. One might get a spear good for hunting on the Sound; another, an arrow for the woods; another, gambling sticks.

Women said they got their basketry designs from ts!a'q. Men with this

---

[219] This is still one of the most popular dances. I have seen it twice at dances held on the Swinomish Reservation where Johnny Fornsby owns a pair of boards. His boards are the same size. They are a plain cross encircled in an oblong band of wood with slightly rounded corners.

spirit had success in hunting and fishing, but they had to do it themselves, for ts!a'q was not as powerful as yilbī'x", who made the animals drop dead.

t!ata'lbix": This spirit could be obtained by both men and women. It helped the former in hunting and the latter in making good mats and baskets.

sqaqkā'gwał, sqa"k!gwał, sqā'gwał: This was a group of three spirits, the first two being men and the third a woman, who were helpful to men and women in industrial pursuits, hunting and preventing illness. sqaqkā'gwał was the eldest and most powerful. sqā"k!gwał was the weakest and was called "he does not always tell the truth." sqā'gwał travelled around the world, walking. This spirit also helped in gambling. When there was illness in a neighboring tribe, the songs of these spirits were sung to prevent the disease from spreading. All the tribes about Puget Sound knew these spirits.

War spirits:

War spirits were called x"qlē'qwad, and a warrior was dux"qlē'qwad, which meant "mean" people. A person with one of these spirits could lead a war party and be elected war chief.

swō'kwad: Loon. This spirit was powerful in war. It lived in a big rock in deep water. Cashmere told of a Snohomish who acquired this spirit and was told that he would be a great warrior provided he did not cut up the first four enemies and did not stain his hands with blood. He had to roast his first four enemies to death over a fire. It happened that the first enemy he caught was his uncle so he roasted him to death and became a great warrior.

sqaip: This was a powerful war spirit who had no house but travelled all the time. He had no servant, but went out himself to meet youths looking for spirits. When a boy saw sqaip he found the spirit painted red all over his head and body. sqaip said to him, "You will be a great fighter; when you dance take a knife and cut yourself and show how powerful you are. Look at me! I'm all red; that is not paint, it is blood. These wounds do not hurt me. You will be the same."

A man possessing this spirit showed his strength by eating dogs and by dancing on fire. sqaip also appeared to women. When a woman had this spirit she was almost like a man. She also danced on fire.

sqaip was not only good in war, but helped in every-day life too.

tōbcā'dād: This spirit was good for war only. It always lived near the salt water and was never found in the mountains. Sometimes a man had to dive for it, but often he would meet it on the beach. In travelling around the world tōbcā'dād flies. He has human form except for wings and feathers on his head. tōbcā'dād always carried a war spear and when a man got this spear, he was the possessor of the spirit. The man with this spirit had a headdress of eagle, hawk and swan feathers called tc!tcxā"al. They wore this when they went to war and at big potlatches.

tōbcā'dād came to a man only in war time and gave great courage. It was the highest war spirit, much more powerful than sqaip. All the tribes about Puget Sound knew of it.

stɛltā'bl, grizzly bear; stca'tx̣ᵘd, black bear; swā'wa', cougar; p!a'tcɛl, wild cat; xa'xɛlos, coon. This group of spirits were both skaletul and x̣ᵘdab. They were good for curing and for war. A person possessing them could endure bad wounds. All five were related to each other as brothers and cousins and they lived together in one house. They were all great shamans and warriors. Coon was the youngest and always picked quarrels with the others. Ordinarily a person could get only one of the five.

The grizzly bears were Skykomish before the world was changed. Therefore the grizzly bears would never kill Skykomish, even if the man has no grizzly bear spirit. When a Skykomish met a grizzly bear, he sang the grizzly bear spirit songs and the bear would not attack him, but would sing and dance and then go away. When a Skykomish woman met a grizzly bear, she drummed with a stick on the bottom of a coiled basket and sang. A Skykomish would never kill a grizzly bear.

When Little Sam was young, his grandfather wanted him to get the grizzly. bear spirit. He could have done this because he was partly Skykomish. He went to the trail where the grizzly bears pass but none came so Little Sam did not get the spirit.

Spirits for acquiring property:

tᶜ¹uɫmɛx̣ᵘ: This was the most powerful spirit of all. Anybody could try to get it, but very few were successful because it was so hard to obtain. Everything was easy for the possessor of this spirit, especially the gaining of wealth. This spirit had a house.

hēyida and tiō'ɫbax̣ᵘ were two spirits for acquiring wealth which were very much alike; in fact one informant claimed that they were the same. It seems however that tiō'ɫbax̣ᵘ was more unusual than hēyida and was not known to so many tribes. The only tribes with a man who had tiō'ɫbax̣ᵘ were: Snohomish, Suquamish, Duwamish, and a tribe northwest of the Lummi.[220] Any tribe, on the other hand, could get hēyida.

hēyida lived in a large house full of property and had many slaves. He looked like a human being and flew through the air, so that boys seeking him did not have to dive. He travelled about and sent out messengers to find boys of high rank who were seeking spirits. hēyida told a boy that he would become wealthy and would not have to work very much. He gave the boy a song. Then the boy joyfully returned home, where he slept all the time and ate nothing. He did not tell his parents his experience. In his sleep he constantly heard his spirit singing. After three or four days he went out to seek additional spirits.

tio'ɫbax̣ᵘ was also helpful in acquiring property, even more so than hēyida. He also caused neighboring tribes to come with gifts. A man with this spirit often had ten to twelve wives because people from other tribes brought their daughters to marry and expected no bride price for them. He made game drop dead at the door of his devotee, especially at the winter dance time. tio'ɫbax̣ᵘ lived under deep water in a long house and those that sought him had to dive with a stone.

---

[220] Perhaps the Nooksack.

Little Sam secured this spirit through his grandfather who was half Snohomish and half Snuqualmi. This spirit was always inherited from father to son. Little Sam was the ninth generation to have it. The first man who possessed it was latsxqē'dE. He fasted forty days until he was thoroughly cleansed. Then he took a stone and dove in salt water. The stone fell on tiō'łbaxᵘ's house. The spirit showed latsxqē'dE all his wealth and promised it to him. When latsxqē'dE came up the tide rose until it covered Skagit Head and he floated along to Mukilteo. There he slept on the beach for five days. On the sixth day he went home. His mother gave him soup to eat. He vomited the food four times, but the fifth time he could swallow it. Then latsxqē'dE made a net for deer and elk and told his relatives to watch the net. They had never seen anything like it before. When latsxqē'dE swung a stick with a carved elk hoof at one end, the elk came running into the net. His relatives ran up and cut the tendons in the animal's hind legs. With the help of tiō'łbaxᵘ, latsxqē'dE caught whale, seal, sturgeon and salmon. The Swinomish, Skykomish, Skagit and Snuqualmi all heard about latsxqē'dE's wonderful feat and came to see him. He gave them all meat and fish to eat and in return they gave him shell money and hides, so that he became very wealthy. Each tribe gave him two girls as wives until he had twenty wives.

The ancestors of latsxqē'dE were Snuqualmi and Snohomish. His grandfather was xulxo'ls, a Snuqualmi who came from Tolt (tōltxᵘ). This man had two daughters who were both married to latsxqē'dE's father, a Snohomish. So the man of the spirit experience narrated above, is the son of latsxqē'dE and qē'sōlitsa, the daughter of xulxo'ls and a Snohomish woman. This couple had many children, of whom latsxqē'dE was the eldest and sdē'u the youngest. Later the tribes from the north came down and killed all of latsxqē'dE's people. sdē'u secured the stiqā'yu (wolf) spirit in much the same way that latsxqē'dE obtained tiō'łbaxᵘ

q!ᵘoxqEn: There were two spirits by this name, one travelling on land, the other by water in a canoe. They were not powerful, but good for bringing wealth. The water spirit had no house, but travelled around all the time looking for wealth to give to the man who had this power. q!ᵘoxqEn met the seeker himself, for he had no servants. The other spirit who travelled on land had the same powers. A person with this spirit could gain wealth easily, especially by gambling. Miscellaneous spirits:

stiqā'yu, wolf. This spirit brought success in hunting and fishing, and also was good for handling dead bodies. To secure it sdē'u, fasted ten days and then made a raft on which he went out on the lake. When he was well out from shore he put water in his ears and, taking a stone in his hands, dove into the water. He came to the house of stiqā'yu, who taught him to make traps for catching seal, sturgeon, flounders, smelts, salmon and deer. The spirit gave sdē'u a stick with a carved deer hoof at one end. When the daughter of stiqā'yu waved the stick, twenty elks, half bucks and half does, dropped dead before her. After sdē'u came out of the water he slept two days and a night.

Little Sam had this spirit and could hunt deer. Shelton said that Steve, a Snohomish, had the wolf spirit and it helped him handle half decayed bodies. He was hired by rich men to remove the dead bodies of their relatives and put them in new graves.[221] Steve could put decayed flesh in his mouth to show his power. He did not eat it.

sbɛtdaq: This was the only spirit with which one could reach the land of the dead.

sq̇apqa'p: This spirit travelled around the world by walking. Sam Wyaks had it and could show his power by cutting himself and dancing and singing. The wounds did not hurt. Once Cashmere was badly cut all over his body and he thought he was going to die. Sam Wyaks made Cashmere get up while he sang the sqapqa'p songs. Sam said to Cashmere, "You are not going to die; you have spirit power." Cashmere began to dance and sing with Sam and the next day he was well.

cū'bādād: This spirit travelled around the edge of the world, a journey that took all winter. In spring he reached a certain point and sang a different song. This spirit had a house and servants, but he went himself to meet a spirit seeker. A person with cū'bādād could predict sickness and could tell whether there will be any sickness all year around. This spirit is not powerful enough alone to give shamanistic power.

q!ᵘa'xx: This was a very common spirit which even slaves possessed. Most old people had this spirit because it has a good tune and makes its owner happy. Otherwise it had no power.

xwē'kwadi: Thunder spirit. This spirit was a huge bird who, when flying about threw off pieces of flint which were the lightning and could split trees. The thunder spirit was difficult to get and must be sought by diving. It was powerful, but it could not help a wounded warrior. A person possessing this spirit could make it thunder at any time. A Snohomish once told a Skykomish that he had the thunder spirit, but the latter would not believe him. So when the Skykomish was out fishing with a flounder net, the owner of the thunder spirit made it thunder and frightened the fisherman. When a shaman watched the Thunder spirit he flew away.

The Nisqually believed that the thunder spirit lived in a rock. When a person with this spirit was hurt it would thunder and rain.

SʟIa'lqab: This spirit travelled in a canoe. It was the only sklaletut in whose dance the cedar board (gudā'yatci') was used.

Crane spirit: Edward Perceval had a headdress of long black feathers which stood erect from a cap. This belonged to the crane spirit which his grandfather had.

stadō'kub': This spirit travelled around the world by walking.

SHAMANISM

A man might become a shaman by acquiring one or more spirits which were effective in curing illness. Such spirits were called xᵘda'b and could appear to both men and women, although women shamans were comparatively rare and not

[221] See p. 54.

very powerful. A shaman's spirit might be an inanimate object or an animal. The animals which appeared as spirits were, otter, beaver, mountain-lion, hawk, eagle, shark, whale, salmon, trout, dog, snake, lizard, owl, cougar. Animals that did not occur as shaman's spirits were: rat, bluejay and robin. Jules never heard of elk, crow, sun or moon, as shaman's spirits. Once a man asserted that "dark night" was his shamanistic spirit. Black bear, cougar, coon and wildcat were very powerful spirits. These spirits were said "to go both ways," which means that they could be layman's spirits or sklaletut as well shaman's spirits or xᵘda'b. Some shamans had both kinds of spirits.

The shaman's spirits might be good or bad. They did not leave their owners to travel as did the sklaletut, and did not travel around the world. Neither did a shaman get sick at winter dance time as did the owners of sklaletut. He could only become ill through the bad influence of another shaman.

There were two kinds of shamans, according to Shelton: those who sucked in curing and those who cured without touching the patient. The former could also look for souls. Shelton did not know which was the greater. Women could practice either way just like the men. The distinction between the two kinds of shamans depended on the kind of spirits he had and what they had taught him. Even the same spirit might not teach all novices the same methods.

The shamans among the Nisqually had no secret society. They came together only when they were invited to do so by a patient. A shaman would never insist on being called. A sick person might invite several shamans; if the first did not cure him, he would get others. Usually there were only about three prominent shamans in a tribe, so often those of neighboring tribes were called. The Nisqually often went to the Snohomish to invite a famous shaman to perform a cure.

Shamans would go in a war party and fight as regular warriors. They practiced no medicine on the war path. As soon as such an expedition started out the difference between shaman and layman disappeared. A shaman would never be chief, but among the Puyallup and Nisqually a head shaman was often more powerful than the regular chief. Nevertheless, he could not interfere with the authority of the war chief. Sicade's grandfather was head shaman of the Nisqually and went to war in 1855-56 as an ordinary warrior, with no special rights. There was never any rivalry between the head shaman and the regular chief. Shamans did not take on special names.

Among the Nisqually children were forbidden to speak to a shaman more than necessary. They should not know about the affairs of medicine.

A shaman lived in the communal house with his relatives and was often wealthy enough to own the house. When a person was ill, he visited the shaman unless he was too ill to move about; in such case the shaman would go to the patient.

Boys went out to get shamanistic spirits at puberty just as they went in quest of a sklaletut. In fact they could get both kinds of spirits at that time or later in life. When a boy got a shaman's spirit he did not attempt to practice at once, but waited until he had acquired six or more spirits. By that time he would be about twenty-five years old. Then after much practice in curing he would be recognized. Often a shaman was well along in middle life before his powers were recognized. Sally Jackson went out for her spirits as a young girl but did not practice until she was between thirty and forty.

It was dangerous to get a shaman's spirit. Cashmere told of a man who sought a shaman's spirit and two spirits fought for him. Sparks flew. The man became frightened and ran away. He was killed and his body was found, twisted and worm eaten. Had he had the courage to stay through the fight he would have gotten one of the two spirits, but since he was cowardly they killed him.

Shaman's spirits as well as other spirits could be inherited.[222] Sally Jackson, a Nisqually shaman, inherited some of her spirits and acquired others for herself.

Another method of becoming a shaman was for a man to reveal his spirit experience at the age of about forty to fifty. When a boy came home from his spirit quest he never told all that had happened to him, not even to his parents. If he told his entire experience then, a shaman might poison him. So when he was between forty and fifty years old he arranged a ceremonial feast and a potlatch to which all his friends were invited. Then he related the entire experience he had had at puberty. He might end this revelation by proclaiming himself a shaman and begin to practice. Many, however, contented themselves with the ceremoney and never practiced as shamans.

Each shaman used the method of curing which his spirit taught him. Sometimes it took several days to complete a cure. Sally Jackson worked at night only and took eight nights to finish healing her patient. During this period she slept all day and ate nothing at all. When a shaman was healing he sang the songs of his spirit and drummed on his cedar board.

The following were some methods of curing:

1. By sucking, either by putting the mouth directly on the affected part or by sucking through a bone with a hole in it or a cedar stick without a hole. The disease was sucked into the bone or stick.

Sicade saw a shaman from British Columbia treat a man for tuberculosis. He sucked a little worm about three-quarter of an inch long out of the patient's body. The shaman would not let Sicade handle the worm. He killed it and said that these worms ate the lungs, thus causing the disease.

2. By pulling out the sickness with the hands. When the thing which made the patient sick had been pulled out the shaman put it in cold water and showed it to the people.[223]

3. By treating with cold water. The sick person was taken to a stream and the shaman bathed the affected parts with cold water. If the patient was too ill to be moved the cold water was brought in a basket. Sometimes the shaman took cold water into his mouth and squirted it on the sore spot.

4. By touching the sore part. The shaman could heal by touching and gently stroking the affected part.

---

[222] Among the Haida the calling of shaman was hereditary in the family, descending usually from maternal uncle to nephew. Swanton, 38.
[223] Chinook, Boas, (b) 41.

Sally Jackson cured by rubbing her hands over the sore part and making a motion as if throwing away the disease.

5. By bleeding. The shaman would try to get out the bad blood which was causing the illness.

6. By singing the patient's spirit songs. A certain woman was sick and no white doctor could cure her. A shaman told the woman's husband that her spirit was stuck in the mud in the river and had left her. His spirit listened for the spirit song of the woman. When the shaman began to sing the patient's spirit song, she got up and sang with him. She was cured. Cashmere explained that this was a typical case. A shaman after listening to the patient's spirit song through his own spirit could sing the song even if he did not possess the same spirit as his patient.

A shaman never blew smoke on the affected part of the patient.

The power of a shaman's spirit was never used for killing animals, only for human beings. When a warrior became dangerous and too overbearing, the people would become afraid of him and have a shaman secretly kill him with his power. Some shaman also claimed that they could kill other shamans with their power. Little Sam killed another shaman by hanging a rush effigy of this shaman's spirit on a house post. The following day the people found that the shaman had hung himself. Among the Nisqually if a shaman was suspected of having killed someone by magic he himself ran the risk of being killed. Henry Martin's brother killed a shaman for this and the people raised no objection.[224]

A shaman could not help a person wounded in war. The warrior had to depend on the power of his own war spirit for healing his wounds. Shamans never practiced magic with the hair or saliva of a person.

Shamans had the power to restore spirits to persons from whom they had been stolen. He might find a person well bodily, but with soul gone because an enemy had set a trap for it. Cashmere told of a woman who was sick and could not be cured by a white doctor. Finally a shaman found out that some Indians from British Columbia had stolen her spirit. He treated her and succeeded in getting her spirit back. As soon as her spirit came back she recovered.

A shaman could show his power by making a stone or a belt or anything turn into a snake which moved. Cashmere knew a man who, through the power of his shamanistic spirit could make his leather belt twist like a snake. A Nisqually shaman, Luke, showed the power of his spirit by eating a pan of cold ashes. The informant said that it was not Luke who ate the ashes but his spirit. Luke could only do this in the winter. Another shaman cut a piece of flesh out of his side and ate it. There was no trace of a wound. This also could be done only in winter.

Sometimes shamans made traps for hunting and fishing. These were supposed to be more effective than those made by ordinary people. Often the shaman merely supervised the process, as when a salmon fence was being built across a river. He then gave it the benefit of the power of his spirit by chanting over it.

---

[224] The Chinook paid a shaman very generously for secretly taking away an enemy's soul. The shaman risked death in doing it. Boas, (b) 41.

Powerful shamans like Little Sam had a snake or a lizard which they "shot" into people. Little Sam cut the head from a snake or a lizard and after drying kept it in his medicine bag. This bag hung in a secret place away from the house. When the shaman went out to treat a patient he tied the bag around his waist after washing and putting on clean clothes. When Little Sam was doctoring he "shot" the head of the snake into the patient. Another shaman used the beak and claws of a bird as medicine, but this was not as powerful as the snake. If a shaman "shot" his medicine into a person and made him sick, another shaman could cure him by saying who had caused his illness and by pulling the bad spirit out.[225]

Sally Jackson had a meeting place in the back of her living house. There she had a large flat pole about ten feet long which represented her spirit. There was no carving on the pole and no painting, except while in use, when it was painted red. The pole was stuck in the ground next to the door. Long poles were used to knock against the ceiling while a treatment was going on. These were painted with red and black stripes across the wide part.

Sicade stated that shamans had clubs which at times became alive and knocked against the ceiling of their own accord. The Nisqually shaman had a rattle made of small deer hoofs. The Nisqually shaman, as most shamans of other tribes, used medicine boards. There were cedar boards which were drummed on with sticks. The Snohomish shaman used no drums. He beat time with a little stick while singing. The people who sang with him also had one or two of these sticks.

Shamans were always paid for their service and often became very rich. A person, if he had been cured, might give his daughter to the shaman as a wife. A slave might also be given in payment. A Nisqually shaman was given a certain amount of property before attempting a treatment. If he was unsuccessful he had to return it. Among the Snohomish if a person died, the shaman would have to return one half of the payment the patient had made. In many cases if the property was not returned by an unsuccessful shaman the people might threaten him with death. There are contradictory statements as to whether this threat was ever executed. It was specified by one informant that women shamans were seldom killed.

List of Shamanistic Spirits (xᵘda'b). stā'dōx!wa': This is the most powerful shaman's spirit. It occupies the same place as tiō'łbaxᵘ does among the layman spirits, the sklaletut. It lived in a house with a fence intended to prevent other shamanistic spirits from entering. This spirit looked like a human being. A shaman who possessed stā'dōk!wa' did not cure by sucking; he simply stood on the opposite side of the house and stretched out his hands toward his patient, making a motion as if reaching out for the disease. In this way he pulled out the disease.

qa'ldwēs: This spirit was next in power. The same data that applies to stā'dōk!wa' also holds for qa'ldwēs.

---

[225] Chinook, Boas, (b) 41.

aya'hōs: This spirit was next in power to qa'ldwēs. He lives up in the air like a bird and can see in all directions. He had two horns on his head, which could be pulled in like a snail's. When angry, he projected them. aya'hōs was large, about the size of an elk, which he also resembled in appearance. A person who met this spirit when he was lost, was apt to die. A hunter once followed the tracks of a fawn and later saw it was aya'hōs. Soon afterwards he died.

qatqā'tc, the red-headed woodpecker, was a powerful spirit. An uncle of Cashmere's father who had it told Cashmere about it, sent him out for it. After fasting a few days Cashmere saw a woodpecker rapping on some rotten wood. Cashmere went up to the bird and tried to catch it but the woodpecker flew away, telling him he still had something in his stomach. Had Cashmere been able to catch the woodpecker he would have become a great shaman.

tcatx, kingfisher, was just a small spirit. It was the least important one that Little Sam had. Once a Neah Bay woman with a powerful spirit seized Little Sam's kingfisher spirit while they were out hop picking. Little Sam became ill; he vomited and spit blood. The woman came to him asking what the trouble was, saying she did not want to kill him. She gave his spirit back to him and he recovered at once. Later Little Sam "shot" his kingfisher spirit into this woman's little boy and killed him. After that Little Sam killed the woman herself with the same spirit.

k!ik!ia'dē', was a variety of small fish. This was the first spirit that Little Sam found. He was lost in the woods and had been without food for several days, when he found his little fish that talked to him and gave him his spirit. Little Sam helped a woman who had trouble in childbirth with this spirit. He forced his little fish down her intestines and pushed the child out. He could also produce an appetite in a sick person by putting this fish into his stomach.

yi'lqē'd was a double headed snake, ten feet long and very thin in the middle. When Little Sam saw this snake it was surrounded by a large number of other snakes who were all its slaves and children. They were coiled up in four piles. Little Sam jumped over these piles of snakes and grasped yi'lqē'd. Then he slept with the snake for two days and two nights. In this way he obtained the spirit.

t!aba'qwap or tɛbā'k!wab, a spirit described by Cashmere as a half snake, having a head but no tail. It was a powerful spirit, always fighting. Hunters often heard t!aba'qwap cry out in the forest but never saw it. It was obviously a mythical being. Little Sam described it further as having four legs. He acquired this spirit at the same time he got the badger sklaletut. Once Little Sam was stabbed with a knife close to his heart. It was this spirit that saved his life. It also helped him cure an insane girl by getting her soul back.

DREAMS

Any person can have a dream that means something. A shaman's spirit is not necessary for dreaming, but a shaman's dreams are more important. Neither does a person have to have a shaman's spirit to interpret a dream or predict from it. A shaman interprets his own dreams just like those of lay people. A person's soul is not ordinarily in the land of the dead when he dreams. If however, he dreams that his soul is going to the land of the dead, it is a very "bad" dream.

When a shaman dreams that his spirit is on the trail to the land of the dead, he can, after he awakens, tell who is going to die soon.

GHOSTS AND SOULS

Every person whether he had a sklaletut or not became a ghost (skayū́) at death. The ghosts lived in the west, across a river (giveɬskayū́stṓlakᵘ). There were two roads leading to the land of the dead, a short one to the left, and a longer one to the right.[226] The latter was travelled by a person who had been sick for a long time. The short road was travelled by those who died suddenly. The ghosts had to cross two rivers, the first very swift, which was bridged over by a fallen tree. The side from which the ghosts approached the second river was low. The farther side had a high bank on which the ghosts lived. This river was crossed in a canoe. When it was low tide on earth it was high tide in the land of ghosts.[227]

A person may die and come to life again in a few days. Little Sam died when he was a boy. He was wrapped in blankets but not buried. He went to the land of ghosts. When he came to the second river he saw the ghosts on the opposite bank. There were many children playing shinny. He wanted to join them. He called to his dead brother to get him. They sent a canoe over and brought him to the land of the ghosts. When he got there the people asked him, "Does your mother know you came here?" Little Sam said, "No." The ghosts told him to go back, for they did not want him now, but he could come back when he was older. He awoke and heard his mother calling him.

Ghosts lived the same kind of life as do the people on earth.[228] Their houses were the same and they hunted and fished. When they walked, their legs crossed constantly. Ghosts travelled, but not around the world like a sklaletut. They sang their songs while travelling. They haunted the house after death. For this reason the belongings of the deceased were put in the canoe with the corpse. To chase the ghost away a large fire was built and the remaining property was burned. If a ghost wanted something that had not been given him he lingered around the house. The dead were put in graveyards away from the village and people avoided the place lest a ghost should get them and make them sick. Ghosts only came at night and never when the moon was shining.

If the sklaletut spirit of a person went to the land of ghosts the person became sick and the sbɛtɛtda′q shamans tried to get the spirit back.

When a person died his soul (sɛli′) went to the land of ghosts. The dead of the various tribes had separate places in the land of the ghosts. The Snohomish did not believe in retribution, but a person took his evil reputation with him. There was no conception of the ghost travelling in the canoe in which he was buried.

---

[226] The Chinook also have two trails leading to the country of the ghosts. If a soul of a sick person takes the one to the left, it means death; the one to the right means recovery. Boas, (b) 39.

[227] For special arrangements for slave, see Slavery, p. 57.

[228] Chinook, Boas, (b) 42, 43.

BIBLIOGRAPHY

BANCROFT, H. H. Native Races of the Pacific States, vol. 1.

BOAS, FRANZ. (a) Ethnology of the Kwakiutl (Thirty-fifth Annual Report, Bureau of American Ethnology, p. 1, Washington, 1921).

(b) Chinook Texts (Bulletin, Bureau of American Ethnology, 20, Washington, 1894).

(c) Kathlamet Texts (Bulletin, Bureau of American Ethnology, 26, Washington, 1901).

(d) Tsimshian Mythology (Thirty-first Annual Report, Bureau of American Ethnology, Washington, 1916).

British Association for the Advancement of Science. Physical Characters, Language, Industrial and Social Conditions of the Northwestern Tribes of the Dominion of Canada (Report, 1890).

CULIN, STEWART. Games of the North American Indians (Twenty-fourth Annual Report, Bureau of American Ethnology, Washington, 1907).

EELLS, MYRON. (a) The Twana, Chemakum and Clallam Indians of Washington Territory (Report, Smithsonian Institution for 1886-1887, 605-681, Washington, 1889).

(b) The Indians of Puget Sound (American Antiquarian and Oriental Journal, 9, 1887, 1-9).

(c) The Puget Sound Indians (Ibid, 211-219).

(d) Decrease of Population among the Indians of Puget Sound (Ibid, 271-276).

FARRAND, LIVINGSTON. Traditions of the Quinault (Publications of the Jesup North Pacific Expedition, 2, Leiden, 1902).

GIBBS, GEORGE. (a) Tribes of Western Washington and Northwestern Oregon (Contributions to North American Ethnology, 1, Washington, 1877).

(b) Report on the Indian Tribes of the Territory of Washington (Pacific Railroad Report, 1, Washington, 1855, 402-436).

GUNTHER, ERNA. (a) Klallam Ethnography (University of Washington Publications in Anthropology, 1927, no. 5).

(b) A Further Analysis of the First Salmon Ceremony (Ibid, 2 1928, no. 5).

Handbook of American Indians (Bulletin, Bureau of American Ethnology, 30, Washington, pt. 1, 1907; pt. 2, 1910).

HATT, GUDMUND. Moccasins and their Relation to Arctic Footgear (Memoirs, American Anthropological Association, 3, 1916).

HOUGH, WALTER. Fire Making Apparatus in the United States National Museum (Report, United States National Museum, 1888).

JEWITT, JOHN R. A Narrative of the Adventures and Suffering of John R. Jewitt (Middletown, 1815).

KANE, PAUL. Wanderings of an Artist among the Indians of North America (London, 1859).

LEWIS, ALBERT B.	Tribes of the Columbia Valley (Memoirs, American Anthropological Association, 1, 1905-1907).

LOWIE, ROBERT H.	The Northern Shoshone (Anthropological Papers, American Museum of Natural History, 2, New York, 1909).

POWERS, STEPHEN.	Indians of California (Contributions to North American Ethnology, 3, Washington, 1877).

SWAN, JAMES G.	(a) The Northwest Coast (New York, 1857).
	(b) The Indians of Cape Flattery (Smithsonian Institutions, Contributions to Knowledge, no. 220, Washington, 1869).

TEIT, JAMES.	The Lillooet Indians (Publications of the Jesup North Pacific Expedition, 2, pt. 5, Leiden, 1906).
	(b) The Thompson Indians (*Ibid*, 1, 1898-1900).

WATERMAN, T. T. and COFFIN, GERALDINE.	(a) Types of Canoes on Puget Sound (Indian Notes and Monographs, Museum of the American Indian, Heye Foundation, New York, 1920).
	(b) Native Houses of Western North America (Indian Notes and Monographs, Museum of the American Indian, Heye Foundation, New York, 1921).

WILLOUGHBY, CHARLES.	Indians of the Quinault Agency (Washington Territory Annual Report, Smithsonian Institution, 1886, 267-282).

WISSLER, CLARK.	(a) Material Culture of the Blackfoot Indians (Anthropological Papers, American Museum of Natural History, 5, New York, 1910).
	(b) Structural Basis to the Decoration of Costumes among the Plains Indians (*Ibid*, 17, 1916).

YARROW, H. C.	A Further Contribution to the Study of the Mortuary Customs of the North American Indians (First Annual Report, Bureau of American Ethnology, Washington, 1881).

Census of 1910.	Indian Population of the United States and Alaska, 1910 (Bureau of Census, Washington, 1915).

PLATE 1. (A). Salmon Heads on Drying Tongs and Clams Set Out to Dry. See p. 22.
(B). Sgᵘdi'lātc Boards Belonging to Johnny Fornsby, Swinomish. See p. 70.
(C). Mrs. Joshua, Snuqualmi Woman, Spinning Mountain Goat Wool. See p. 31.
(D). House Post of an Old Potlatch House near Tulalip, Showing Notched Upright and Fitted Cross Beam. See p. 15.

PLATE 2. (A). Annie Sam, a Snuqualmi, Wife of Little Sam, One of Dr. Haeberlin's Principal Informants. See p. 51.

(B). William Shelton, a Snohomish.

(C). Drying Cattail Rushes to be Used for Mats. See p. 32.